Called to Testify

The First Christian Witnesses

KENNETH KREMER

Northwestern Publishing House
Milwaukee, Wisconsin

To Kati, Jack, Ryan, Madelyn, and Owen—
that you may always know Jesus
as intimately as those who live
within the pages of this book.

Cover illustration by Terry Julien

Scripture is taken from the HOLY BIBLE, NEW INTERNATIONAL VERSION®. Copyright © 1973, 1978, 1984 by International Bible Society. Used by permission of Zondervan Publishing House. All rights reserved.

The "NIV" and "New International Version" trademarks are registered in the United States Patent and Trademark Office by International Bible Society. Use of either trademark requires the permission of International Bible Society.

Library of Congress Control Number: 2003101634
Northwestern Publishing House
1250 N. 113th St., Milwaukee, WI 53226-3284
www.nph.net
© 2003 by Northwestern Publishing House
Published 2003
Printed in the United States of America
ISBN 0-8100-1560-9

Contents

---------- **Introduction** ----------

Not long ago I received a subpoena in the mail. It was for a civil case. I was being called as a witness. I might have tossed the document out in the trash, but the important language caught my eye. It was worded carefully. I did not have a choice. I was required to appear. My testimony was scheduled to be read into the court record as evidence. I decided to take the summons seriously.

You and I have been called as witnesses. In the washing of Baptism, we have each also received our subpoenas.

Most of us get shaky in the knees at the thought of having to appear in court. Before you have an anxiety attack, consider this: Everyone branded with Jesus' name has received a similar summons. We join an endless throng of witnesses, always giving glory to God's name with our eyewitness accounts. We share in the honor with the likes of Abraham, Moses, Ruth, David, and Elijah; the apostles Peter, John, and Paul; and many more of the saints. So also do the men and women whose names were never recorded for posterity—the John and Jane Does of Scripture—shepherds, felons, soldiers, prostitutes, lepers, tax collectors. This book presents the testimonies of nine unnamed individuals whose lives intersected with the Savior's, if only briefly. It is a journey into their lives and what they might say about their encounters with Jesus. I hope you enjoy meeting them as much as I have.

In reconstructing their testimonies, careful attention was given to the Scriptures. The purpose was not to add to or subtract from inspired words. God warns us not to try to improve on divine truth. But an eyewitness account is, by definition, deeply personal. That is what makes it so compelling. Testimony is always shaped by a witness' unique perspective. Personal experiences, attitudes, culture, and beliefs all play a role.

The Bible does not often provide commentary on what people thought or felt. That involves speculation. In general terms, we can presume to understand how a leper might feel or think; some emotions are universal to all human experience. But we cannot know with any degree of certainty what that solitary and grateful tenth leper felt when he discovered that Jesus had cleansed his body of the terrible disease. To attempt to describe what he felt or thought, as this book does, is pure fiction.

There are risks involved in probing the edges of *what if*. Some are worth taking; others are not. Why take the risks? In first-person accounts, we get a rare glimpse of our own stories. We inevitably conclude that the experiences of others are not so different from our own.

There is another reason to rehearse the testimonials of God's called witnesses when Scripture only hints at them. In a celebrated article entitled "God in the Dock," C. S. Lewis points to a profound shift that occurred during his half of the twentieth century: "The ancient man approached God (or even the gods) as the accused person approaches his judge. For the modern man the roles are reversed; [man] is the judge: God is in the dock" (*The Collected Works of C. S. Lewis*, New York: Inspiration Press, 1996, p. 464).

If Lewis was right in 1947, his observation is even more astute for the postmodern world. Man has maneuvered himself onto the judgment seat; God is in the dock, under investigation and subject to critical questions. How far our race has drifted from its loving Creator! By the same token, little has changed from that night 2,000 years ago when an illegally called Sanhedrin met in Jerusalem in the middle of the night. God was in the dock then as well.

In one sense, God has always been on trial. " 'Test me in this,' says the LORD Almighty, 'and see if I will not throw open the flood-

gates of heaven and pour out so much blessing that you will not have room enough for it.' "[1] From the beginning, he has invited us to put him to the test. He has placed his own promises into evidence. Down through history, one by one the witnesses step forward. Each provides another aspect, another view, another experience, adding to the testimony. A corpus of evidence is gathered, creating, as it were, the whole truth and nothing but the truth. The case is profoundly compelling: God is faithful. The eternal court record bears witness to his unfathomable grace and goodness. You and I are there. Our statements are part of the grand record, for we too have been called to testify.

[1]Malachi 3:10

"Come and listen, all
you who fear God;
let me tell you what
he has done for me."

Psalm 66:16

An infant, sleeping on a mattress of fresh hay.
A happy young woman and her proud husband.
Cattle, bellowing. A donkey. Not far off in the distant
night, shepherds approach, lambs collared about their
shoulders to share body warmth against the cool night air.
An event so commonplace that most thought of it as
unimportant. Yet for us that night has unmatched
significance. Christians the world over agree: everything
changed on the holy night when God's plan began to
flower in an ancient Bethlehem grotto. If centuries later
one of those shepherds were to testify to what he saw and
heard, our ears would tingle with his story.

Sudden Peace[2]

You ask me to tell the story of that night. It makes all other stories seem pale and unimportant. I have never stopped telling it. My heart still beats a little faster with each telling. The story itself is ancient, but it has never become old. I will tell it to you just as I have told it to many others.

To begin, I did not imagine that night or make it up. How could I imagine something so astonishing? I am a shepherd, not a learned man like the scribes or priests. Most people think we are dull and a little stupid. But we are no duller or slower than any other people. Nor are we fools. Yet we are not so gifted to be able to concoct a story like this. I must impress on you that whatever happened that night was real. We were not drunk. This was not a vision. My mind and heart—I speak for myself now—were more alert and active than ever before. The ancient Scriptures raced through my thoughts with blinding speed. I may not have comprehended all that was happening, but I immediately recognized its great significance. And I know that if you were to ask them, the others would support me in my testimony.

My companions have used the word *beautiful* to describe the events of that night. I would not disagree. One of the prophets wrote, *"How beautiful on the mountains are the feet of those . . . who bring good tidings, who proclaim salvation, who say to Zion, 'Your God reigns!' "*[3] But this was the kind of beauty that penetrates

[2]Luke 2:1-20
[3]Isaiah 52:7

the soul; it can only be beautiful if everything is right with the world and justice prevails.

There are many other words that summarize my own thoughts and feelings. *Joy* is the first that comes to mind. Yes, much joy! But there was also the element of *surprise.* It all happened with such suddenness—with the forcefulness and urgency of a pregnant ewe birthing a lamb. In an instant the dark night sky burst into light as if the sun had returned or someone suddenly pulled back a curtain. I stood there, bathed in the light of my eternal future. Nothing could have prepared me for that moment. I was like Moses, shielding myself from the Almighty's all-consuming brilliance. Light flowed from every direction. Brilliant light. Divine light. As much internal as external. Like life itself. I could have been blind, and I still would have "seen" it. It was warm on my skin; I could taste it. It was that powerful. It filled me with a sense of unrestrained awe . . . and unrelenting terror.

Courage is essential in the character of a shepherd. I myself have stared death in the face and never flinched. Edomites—the uncircumcised heathens—often raided our flocks, stealing the fattest ewes and heartiest rams to improve their inferior stock. A good shepherd is ready to defend his flock with his life. But that night I knew terror I will never forget. My heart pounded. The flocks remained calm, yet I was paralyzed with fear. I wanted to run, but only my mind was able to move. And it was reeling, searching for a prayer or words from Scripture, anything to relieve the terror of the moment.

I remembered a psalm: *"The LORD is my light and my salvation—whom shall I fear? The LORD is the stronghold of my life—of whom shall I be afraid?"*[4] It was all I could think of. It was all I needed. David's poetry helped me find peace and strength.

God's holy messenger further quieted my racing heart. "Do not be afraid," said the gentle voice. Afraid, I stood like a stone.

You may wonder, "What did this angel of the Most High look like?" I cannot say. I was too frightened to get a good

[4]Psalm 27:1

look. His presence was large, looming above us. And the angel's voice resonated as much within the bones and sinews of my body as it echoed across the valley to the distant hills. In hindsight, the messenger's actual countenance seems unimportant. (Men foolishly lose sleep over such things.) With the angel's words, my terror disappeared into the night. Somehow I knew that everything was possible. It was good, *very good*, just as the Almighty's creation was all *very good* in the beginning.

Then, for a miserable shepherd whom the Almighty could have forgotten from birth, what happened next was even more sudden. The messenger spoke again, like a town herald crying out *"All is well"* into the dark, uncertain night.

"This very night," said the messenger, "in David's village, the Anointed One—Christ—was born of a woman."

This was the news for which every Jew had been yearning. Liberating news! History-making news! Radical news! Unexpected yet long-awaited news! The centuries of waiting were over. And I was there—me, a penniless, good-for-nothing, smelly peasant of a shepherd.

I was beside myself with a thousand emotions. And yet, I wonder why. Did we not expect the ancient writings to be true? They were written by the prophets. I was reminded from childhood that I hailed from Bethlehem. Every kid in the region committed Micah's words to memory: *"But you, Bethlehem Ephrathah, though you are small among the clans of Judah, out of you will come for me one who will be the ruler over Israel. . . . And he will be their peace."*[5] How could we have been so thickheaded? There were plenty of signs. Hadn't the prophet made it clear when he wrote: *"To us a child is born, to us a son is given. . . . And he will be called Wonderful Counselor, Mighty God, Everlasting Father, Prince of Peace"*?[6]

Of course! And now the Lord's spokesman provided details that would make it impossible for us to miss our divine Prince. "Go. Look for the child," said the messenger. "He will be wrapped in cloth strips and cradled in a feeding trough."

[5]Micah 5:2,5
[6]Isaiah 9:6

It was a personal invitation: Come, and be the Lord's witness.

Each of us had already decided what must be done. But before any of us could act, the night sky glowed brighter than daylight. And a choir of heavenly beings joined the Lord's messenger. Their voices filled the air with a song so tender that we could no longer hold in what we felt. Tears of joy streamed down our leathery cheeks.

Besides my own untrained voice, a shepherd's lute and skin drum are the only musical instruments I have ever heard. But I know what pleases my ears. This melody was composed in heaven. Like fragrant wisps of incense, it wafted upward, outward, extending to the plains and mountains and oceans, far beyond our little paddock. The rhythms of this muse pulsed with the heartbeat of life, alternately shaking the earth like thunder and mimicking the songs of birds. *"Glory,"* sang the host. Over and over. I would have gladly stayed there for all of eternity. *"Glory to God in the highest, and on earth peace to men on whom his favor rests."*[7] I recognized it; I had heard it before, or something like it, as had every Jew. Similar words were spoken by Aaron in the desert: *"The LORD bless you and keep you; the LORD make his face shine upon you and be gracious to you; the LORD turn his face toward you and give you peace."*[8] It was a blessed *shalom* from the heavenly Father.

This was the gift! Peace. "My peace forever dwells within your hearts because you are my people and I AM your God. I live among you now in the flesh of an infant—a son of man—my Son." I might add, this was a gift that I never knew I wanted or needed, not until that moment. Then suddenly I treasured it with all my being. You may have heard that a good shepherd will risk his entire flock to search for a single wayward lamb. On this night of nights, I was that lamb. My Shepherd had come, seeking me. And suddenly I had no other wants or needs in life, only him. I rested beside his quiet waters, refreshed, filled, satisfied, and at peace.

[7]Luke 2:14
[8]Numbers 6:24-26

We left our sheep, confident that all was well, and went into town looking for our little King. The Prince of all *shaloms* had arrived. Such a revelation was too compelling to stay and do nothing. But the haste in which we now conducted our search was a bit out of character for shepherds. How foolish we must have looked! We are a people known to do nothing in a hurry. We fell all over each other to be the first to lay eyes on the miracle child.

For the past few weeks, the dusty road leading into Bethlehem had been busy with sojourners, making their way in and out of the village. The Romans had said that everyone must be counted according to clan. The crowds meant that more Roman coins were in circulation. Times were good. But all the inns were filled with travelers. The child's parents would have had to seek shelter from the night. But where? I had some ideas.

The Lord's messenger had said we would find the child in a surprisingly ordinary place. We did. The newborn was swaddled in strips of linen cloth and bedded on a pile of straw.

I have the picture fixed forever in my mind's eye. There are only two figures of any real consequence in view. The first figure is the child—silently sleeping with cattle and sheep milling about. I stood there for a while in wonder. Finally I gathered the will to ask a question. "His name?" I whispered.

"Jesus," was the hushed reply from the infant's proud father. "It means, *the Lord saves.*" Those were the only words spoken that night in the stable. I fell to my knees, overcome with gratitude and awe, and I adored the little Prince from heaven.

I said there were *two* figures in my living impression of that night. The second is *me*. The Holy One's favor had surely rested on me that night; his face was shining so brightly that I must have been glowing inside and out. People say I am glowing to this very day. The Lord's messenger had said this news meant great joy *to all people*. I counted myself among that flock.

What I have testified to has been told and retold for two thousand years. It will forever be a sudden, unexpected redemption, delivered in the night of hopeless despair—the surprise of the ages. This night the gates of heaven were forever flung open. I will never forget that.

My friends and I left hooting like festive pilgrims. We awakened the town's people with our celebrating. Then they too learned of the unexpected events of that night. We told them of the birth of this Hebrew Son. They heard our testimony and were left pondering its meaning.

When dawn began to break, our little band could be heard in the distance, singing the psalm of the ancient shepherd-king:

"I will exalt you, my God the King;
I will . . . extol your name for ever and ever.
Your kingdom is an everlasting kingdom,
and your dominion endures through all generations."[9]

---

[9]Psalm 145:1,2,13

Weddings are always memorable events.
Every culture can relate to that emotional moment when
a man and woman are bound together in marriage.
In the Bible this relationship appears as a metaphor for the
relationship between Christ and his church.
Wedding feasts served as the settings for several of the
parables that Jesus told in order to teach a truth.
Weddings are unique celebrations. They commemorate the
first time that a bride and groom publicly pledge
their faithfulness to each other and promise
to love each other throughout their life on earth.

The experience of the young bride that follows bears
witness to another significant first—the first sign in Jesus'
public life demonstrating his glory. Her testimony gives
hope to those who look for a miracle to occur in their lives.

The First Sign[10]

Who are we to pretend that we know the mind of the Almighty? I should have known better than to abandon hope. But, in my case, the Almighty would have had to accomplish the impossible. So, already at an early age, I had resigned myself to a horrible destiny.

Life without a partner is a rare thing in Jewish culture. It is also a fate worse than being a widow. A social stigma shadowed women who never married. That was the bleak and lonely future I faced. I would surely embrace poverty and spend life on the fringe of society. I was convinced this was my future. Now I like to think that I was brave about it, but I was not always as brave as I like to imagine.

When the other girls of my village were betrothed, no one teased me about the day when I too might be matched with some fine, young man. When my four younger sisters wed, they were careful not to bruise my feelings by suggesting that my turn would someday come. Their eyes told them that was unlikely. I did not have a single feature to attract the attentions of a suitor. I was hideously ugly. Nor did I need to be told the unhappy truth. The old men of Cana groaned and turned their heads in pity as I passed them on my way to the well. The young men pretended I did not even exist, then snickered when my back was turned. I was cursed with a face permanently fixed in an angry expression. Try as I might to overcome the image, my countenance failed to communicate joy or

[10]John 2:1-11

warmth to others. And though I prayed fervently about my plight, I wondered in my heart what man would ever want to spend his life with a woman who scowled at him whenever he looked at her.

My father tried to lighten my burden. He made jokes to relieve the pressure. "After the marriages of four other daughters, I have nothing left to offer as a *mohar*,[11]" he would say. Then he would laugh.

I knew better. Father was careful with his money. I knew that he was quietly trying to yoke me with some eligible man. Poverty was not the problem; desirability was. In a marketplace where a woman's ability to bear sons and carry out her domestic responsibilities ranked high, physical appearances hardly mattered. Still, there was little hope for someone as uncomely as I.

I wasn't getting any younger either. I had almost accepted the whole sad situation. I say *almost* because in my weaker moments, I permitted myself to dream of some ugly troll-of-a-man desperate enough to take me for a wife.

As things turned out, it was not my countenance at all that held my future in suspense. It was God's timing, which, I might add, was quite impeccable. Just when I was about to abandon all hope, my father came to me to tell me that he had negotiated a union. His expression was all serious and patronizing. I almost laughed as he spoke. But a shard of light twinkled so brightly in his eye that I knew he was delighted. Of course, always the tease, he made the most of the moment, stammering and hawing before telling me that it was Reuben I was to wed.

In my eyes Reuben was no toad of a man. He was a worthy catch! It took a moment for me to grasp the fullness of this unexpected blessing. Reuben had a fine reputation. He held a prominent position in the synagogue. He was known as a shrewd businessman, but honest. He was strong, robust, witty, and better than ordinary in appearance. My cup was overflowing! I consented.

---

[11]The *mohar* was the Jewish version of a dowry—a sum of money or property used to negotiate a contract marriage. Accordingly, the fathers of both the bride and the groom served as brokers in the betrothal process.

Word spread quickly that my father was about to make a public announcement. Soon neighbors and relatives surrounded the entrance to our house. They speculated that Father had successfully engineered my betrothal.

Mother encouraged me, saying that my joy was glowing from within. I was proud to step out into the sunlight, and I did not care if others grimaced at my looks. Reuben apparently did not; he saw me in a different light. And I was ever so grateful.

My father spoke first. He already had plenty of practice. His voice boomed as he heaped honor on Reuben's family. I thought his speech was a bit overdone but felt warm inside to see how proud he was with the match he had made.

Then Reuben's father spoke. He said our two families were now also joined in a common bond through this marriage. This pleased him. Then he introduced Reuben.

As Reuben stepped into the middle of the circle of friends and relatives, he was greeted with cheers and hoots of jubilation. Some of his closest friends joined together in singing the chorus of a psalm. It was then that I first saw Reuben's humility. It was difficult for him to raise his eyes to meet the admiring gazes of our guests.

I had known Reuben from childhood, though not very well. He was older, 12 years to be exact. Once, when I was a child, he befriended me. I have forgotten the circumstances but not his kindness. As he spoke now, I recalled the gentle voice that consoled me in my childhood distress. I knew I could love this man.

His hands trembled. So did his voice. He struggled to maintain his composure. This was an important day in his life, as it was in mine. He read from a parchment—words written by his own hand. He spoke from a pious heart: "I came to your house so that you might give me your daughter's hand in marriage and to make this declaration public, before my friends, my dear family members, and the Almighty's throne." He stopped to clear his throat, unaccustomed to speaking in public. "This is my intent: . . ." Then he raised his voice and shouted: "From this day and forevermore, she is my bride, and I am her groom.

She is my wife, and I am her husband. She is my joy, and *in her
my joy shall be complete."*

A shout arose that sounded like we had just won a great battle. Before God and man it was done. The miracle of my life
had just happened; a man had taken me as his bride. I took it as
a sign that the Almighty still cared for those suspended in
hopelessness. It was the first of many signs.

The days that followed went by quickly. Like any other
bride, my time was consumed in planning. Reuben and I saw
little of each other. I was thankful for the veil, which, according
to tradition, I now always used to cover my face. (I still feared
that Reuben might reconsider, if he ever came to his senses.)

My anticipation grew with each passing day. I began to
experience the giddy joy of looking forward to being physically
together with a man whom I respected with all my heart. There
were so many firsts to anticipate. Soon I even found myself
being comfortable with the idea of living in another man's
house, bearing his children, and serving him in humble joy.

I barely slept the night before the wedding. I wanted it to
be memorable not for the foul-ups and unintended offenses
that sometimes scar these fragile family affairs but for our
generosity and grace. Then the morning sun filled the sky
with a cherry glow, and my anxiety vanished as on the wings
of an eagle.

My sisters began bustling about with no small amount of
energy and urgency. Sleep was out of the question. One
primped and manicured. Another perfumed. A third fitted me
with the wedding garment. Then my youngest sister adorned
me with the beautiful gifts of jewelry Reuben sent in my honor.
They oohed and aahed like adolescents, saying that Reuben
would no longer be the only man to see how desirable I was.
No one had ever said such a thing to me before. They wove a
floral headpiece into my hair and walked me to the litter that
awaited just outside the door.

Our friends and relatives had been gathering most of the
day. They followed us through the narrow streets of Cana,
making a clamor as though they were hailing the Queen of

Sheba. I sat straight and tall and imagined that I ruled my loyal subjects with justice and mercy.

In the distance I could hear Reuben and his entourage winding its way through Cana's back streets. They were headed in our direction. He too would be carried on a litter, decked in garlands with ceremonial "armed guards" at his side—my conquering hero! Their jubilant mood equaled ours. Closer we moved to that arranged place where the groom would eagerly await my regal arrival. Then suddenly Reuben was there, and I was joining him on his litter, no longer under my father's authority or care.

Later that night my husband and I would consummate our union. For now, in the eyes of God and man, the two of us were already one.

Our exquisite day was to be followed by six more days of food and drink, singing, poetic readings, laughter, warm exchanges, business deals, renewed friendships, intimate glances, and young and old spending time together. And, oh, how many old acquaintances there were to be renewed! And new friends to be made! Some came from as far away as Nazareth. Like Mary. She had made the journey with several other widows. Reuben quickly accepted her offer to manage some of the details of the celebration. What a help she was!

As the feast progressed, it was Mary who first recognized an impending crisis. The wine had dwindled. It was no one's fault. The weather in Cana at this time of year is very hot. The guests drank more wine than expected. And there were many more guests than we had planned. Like Mary's son Jesus, who traveled with a small band of students—Andrew, Peter, Nathaniel, Philip, James, and John. We were happy to have the young rabbi come by to bless our union, but his presence put a strain on our supply of wine. His followers were good men, but thirsty.

Some of our guests had made arrangements to stay with neighboring friends and relatives for the week. They relied on us to provide for their needs. Our local friends and relatives planned to return each evening after their day's work for more celebrating. It would be a terrible offense if our celebration were to abruptly end. But end it would. No cured wine in such a large quantity was to be found anywhere in Cana.

Mary quietly went looking for her son. She must have sensed that Jesus might have a solution. I doubt, though, that she anticipated the wonder that would soon take place. When she found him, I was standing nearby. I overheard the conversation. "They have no more wine," she said discreetly. I could tell she was trying to spare Reuben from learning of the crisis. Her voice betrayed a sense of helpless desperation.

Oh, the tender look in her son's eyes! He paused a long time before responding. How he honored and respected his mother! How he loved her! "Dear woman," he said, "why do you involve me? My time has not yet come."

Mary was not hurt. Rather she smiled, knowing that her son's path was not the path of ordinary men. His path had been ordained long ago. The impeccable timing of the Almighty would now take precedence. She knew that Jesus would deal with the crisis according to his own divine schedule. So she looked about to find some of the servants. "Do whatever he tells you," she told them.

Time passed—enough time that old anxious feelings began to return. This time I watched and waited, confident that the Almighty still cared. He was testing our patience.

Then, as though driven by some divine timepiece, when hope had all but vanished, Jesus told the servants to fill six large jars with water. The jars had been placed near the entrance for the foot-washing ceremony.

The servants followed Jesus' instruction, filling all the jars to the brims.

"Now draw some out," he told them, "and take it to the banquet's master."

The servants did as they were told.

When the banquet master put the cup to his lips and tasted, he was baffled. He had not even been aware of a shortage. Now he was surprised by the fine quality of the wine he had just tested. Normally the best wine is served when guests can still be impressed with excellence. He wondered why the best wine had been held in reserve so long.

Jesus won our hearts that day—Reuben's and mine. Over the next few months, we occasionally heard about the great things he was doing in Galilee and later in Judea. Many miracles followed—more impressive miracles—lepers healed, the dead restored to life, the blind given sight, crippled legs given the strength to walk, demons cast out. But this was the first. It was all we needed to be convinced that he truly is the Son of the Almighty.

We marveled too because Jesus' first miracle took place at a homespun wedding in a dusty, off-the-highway little village in Galilee. Why not Jerusalem? God's Son had come to participate fully in the ordinary affairs of ordinary people. He cared about the mundane, day-to-day events of our lives. He concerned himself with things like tradition and family honor. He cared that we have enough food to eat and wine to drink. He smiled with us when we were happy and frowned with us when we were sad. That is his nature.

Becoming a patient woman turned out to be a lifelong endeavor. Marriage was a good training ground for that. I learned how to wait for the Lord to carry out his will according to his own perfect timetable.

I have also become more conscious of the many little miracles that occur in our day-to-day lives, often in overwhelming abundance. Our water jars were always filled to overflowing with the very best of the Almighty's blessings. If you take the time to look, you will discover the same is true of your life.

As the years passed, the memory of our wedding day faded. That is the way life is. In the end it is the marriage that proves to be far more important than the wedding. I still, however, always looked forward to the eternal banquet—the Groom's victory feast spread in glorious array before his fallen enemies. It's mine, a vision of my future, undeserving and hideous as I might be. Oh, miracle of miracles!

Franklin Delano Roosevelt said that December 7, 1941—
Pearl Harbor Day—was a day that would live in infamy.
We do not forget such events. Many people remember
exactly where they were and what they were doing on
November 22, 1963, when they first heard the news
of JFK's assassination. After the terrorist attacks
of September 11, 2001, nothing would ever
be quite the same. Time seems to meander
at a snail's pace until one of those pregnant
moments comes along that changes everything.

Such moments also occur in the lives of individuals.
We are about to learn of one such moment from the woman
who now takes the witness stand. As we hear her witness,
it is wise to remember the psalmist's words:
"My times are in your hands" (Psalm 31:15).

Life ... Again[12]

You may not appreciate the extremes of the day that I am about to describe. In less than 12 hours, a life so dear was torn from me, then mercifully restored. I can speak about it now. At the time my lips could not keep up with my heart.

The day began as any other day. The sun's morning rays were warm, the air sweet enough to dispel the bitterness of a fitful night. Memories of better times haunted my evening hours.

In spite of all that we were lacking, ours was a happy existence—a proud mother and her devoted son. Our community was a good place to live. People cared, as one might expect in a place called Nain.

Nain was a sleepy little village. Occasionally a stray caravan wandered through, but most of the time, traffic stayed on more familiar roads.

My husband had died several years before. So my son and I only had each other.

We made our way on life's journey together, content with what the Almighty had given us. Life was difficult. But we were never so destitute as to be miserable. Soon my dear son would take his place among the other men of the village, a tradesman, perhaps. A mother could be optimistic. Surely life would improve then. He had a strong body, a steady hand, and a capable mind. He would represent the family name with dignity and integrity. He already was my emotional sustenance—my comfort, my reason for living, and my joy. Especially my joy.

[12]Luke 7:11-17

Do not ask me how I knew. Instinct perhaps. A mother senses when her child is in danger. When I heard the ram's horn, I knew immediately that it was my boy who had just been claimed for eternity. In those first few seconds, time remained suspended. My shattered heart felt as though it was being dismantled piece by piece. "Oh, how fleeting is life," I thought to myself, "our days a mere handsbreath!"

In the fog of information that followed, it became clear that the child to whom I had first given life was the victim of a tragic accident. A part of me refused to acknowledge the fact. It was impossible to digest. Like everyone else, my first reaction was to deny. I remained paralyzed in disbelief, unable to move or speak.

Perhaps God blesses us with confusion at such times. Who can prepare for such news? So he helps us cope by rejecting words, ignoring truth, meeting reality with disbelief. Only when the mind is able to safely navigate into the maze of emotions do we begin the agonizing process of accepting a tragic fact.

A flood of emotions washed over me. But slowly the loss began to burrow inside, settling into a dark corner of my soul. One moment I yearned for those days when we shared our time together. My mind flashed to glorious memories of my son—a sweet, temporary respite. Then the awful truth would return tenfold, pounding the terrible reality home. Oceans of darkness surged over me—wave after wave of the most devastating horror—until, finally, I longed to join the child of my heart in death. I understood now what Solomon meant when he wrote, *"The dead, who had already died, are happier than the living, who are still alive. But better than both is he who has not yet been, who has not seen the evil that is done under the sun."*[13] Grief swallows its victim whole. I wished I had never been born.

You have asked me to say something about the role my son played in my life. Do such words exist? If so, what could they be? How does a mother measure the place she has in her heart for her only child? This son received life from me. He was my dearest treasure, my reason for living. Only a mother can understand that relationship.

[13]Ecclesiastes 4:2,3

In other homes, when death takes a family member, the survivors mourn their loss, bury their dead, remember, and then find a way to go on in life. That would be impossible for me. A childless widow faces the future alone. I would live out my days without his loving smile, his curious conversation, his reassuring voice. I needed him like I needed water or food. Even more, I longed for this son of mine to need his mother. Now there was nothing left to fill the fragile emptiness. How does one then move on?

Friends tried to console me. They whispered heartfelt expressions reserved for such times. They meant well, offering encouragement and hope. They repeated the ancient sayings of the Shekinah—words from the ark of the covenant, where God himself resided. There the name *Jehovah* lives with all its holy authority, power, and mercy.

But smoldering among the wreckage of my emotions lay a heart that was also consumed with anger. I held the Almighty responsible. He permitted this unthinkable tragedy. Where was his Shekinah in the moment of my son's distress? How could a great and loving Jehovah be so cruel? What purpose could he have? I challenged his authority over life and death. I questioned the foolishness of his holy wisdom.

Some will recoil at my outrage. I surely will not be the last. *"My thoughts are not your thoughts,"*[14] declares the Almighty. How true! Yet I remained rooted in the idea that his ways had to conform to my way of thinking. I forgot the distinction between Creator and creature.

I tore at my hair, rent my tunic, and bared the breasts that had given nourishment to my son. I covered my head with ashes from the firepit and flung a handful into the wind, aiming at the object of my anger. Then I collapsed in a pile of inconsolable distress.

A neighbor offered a sackcloth mantle of camel's hair to cover my shame. I did not acknowledge her kindness.

The machinery of tradition quickly put ancient rituals in motion. The wailing began. Friends added their voices from the depths of their own anguish. A cousin spread the general

---

[14]Isaiah 55:8

invitation for everyone in the community to join me in my grief. "Weep with her, all you who are of bitter heart," he cried. A friend of the family followed close behind, piping a sad melody on his flute.

Many people gathered near the house, playing tiny cymbals and bells. They mourned, "Alas, the Lion; alas, the Hero!" A ram's horn trumpeted the news to those working in the distant hills.

Soon the body of my son, broken and lifeless, was brought to our home. I remained at his side, stroking his arms and head, perhaps hoping I could stir his life again. But all it did was make me unclean. I did not care. I suddenly had little interest in the Sabbath or worship. I refused to eat, drink, or to speak to anyone. Instead I turned away, unable and unwilling to share my loss. The prophet's ancient dirge echoed in my heart: *"I sat alone because your hand was on me and you had filled me with indignation. Why is my pain unending and my wound grievous and incurable? Will you be to me a deceptive brook, like a spring that fails?"*[15]

The body was washed, the hair cut, the nails trimmed. Then the corpse was anointed and wrapped in bandages of spice-soaked linen. The "salt of the earth" was spread over the wicker bier that would transport my child to the *house of eternal rest.* His arms were crossed at the wrists. A shroud covered his torso to the neck. But his pale, lifeless face remained exposed so that the living might be reminded that in time they too would relinquish their breaths.

A throng of mourners came to share in my grief. I failed to notice. The procession moved slowly to accommodate those of us who crumbled in a heap of despair every few paces. Some of my son's childhood companions were recruited as pallbearers. They stopped every now and then to exchange places with other young men who wanted to share the burden. Each time we stopped, the lamenting increased. An elder took advantage of these moments to read a homily. He listed the accomplishments of my son's shortened life.

As we passed through the city gates, a second crowd of travelers merged with this procession—one throng, oppressed with

<hr>

[15]a lamentation from Jeremiah 15:17,18

the reality of death; the other, full of life and vitality—like two opposing armies meeting in a skirmish. We stopped. I thought it was to change bearers once more. I did not realize that a young rabbi had halted our progress. I was not, at first, even aware of him, nor did I know *of* him, though others may have. He said nothing. He shed no tears. But he had a look of complete confidence about him.

We stood like statuary, unsure of what to do. Yet the rabbi seemed to know exactly what was about to happen. Tears clouded my sight. When I looked up, I saw a blurred figure approaching—the young rabbi. I expected a word of condolence. It could not make my shattered heart whole again, but coming from a rabbi, such sympathy would be meaningful.

The tears washing down my cheeks must have whispered a wordless prayer. As I wiped my tears aside, I could read the love in his expression. He cared. He intended to address my sadness, though how was still unclear.

"Don't cry anymore," he said. He spoke as though I were the only person within miles. Yet he was speaking to every person who had ever drawn breath. His words seemed to signal an end to all despair, when only moments earlier all had been hopeless.

The holy teacher did not take me to task for the weakness of my faith or lecture me about my anger. Instead, he stepped between two of the pallbearers and placed both of his hands on the pallet where my son's lifeless body lay, defiling himself, undeterred by ancient taboos. I thought to myself, "You would think that a rabbi would be more careful than to approach the dead." But it was a majestic moment; his fearless gesture held great promise.

He leaned over the body, peered into my son's pallid face, and spoke in an airy whisper to the corpse. "Young man," he said, "I say to you, *get up!*" I had said the very same words to wake my son every morning since he was an infant. But since that day, I have relived that moment thousands of times. He who filled Adam's clay lungs with the miracle of life had just ushered his living Spirit into the only offspring of my womb. To all who have ears, let them hear: The Lord, he is Lord over all things. He will not abandon us to the grave, nor will he let his Holy One see decay.[16] I held my breath. Nothing happened for what seemed like a very long time. Then the cadaver's chest began to expand; a rush of air filled its lungs. The chest contracted again, more slowly, expelling air. His eyelids twitched, fluttered, then opened wide, his eyes bright and clear and filled with the light of life.

He gathered himself as though he had just awakened from a satisfying sleep, shifting his weight so that the bearers now had to work at balancing the pallet. The red rouge of life returned to his cheeks and lips.

I had a difficult time making sense of what had just occurred. Dead people don't just throw off the shroud. It is not possible: dead is dead. The shock of new life was as paralyzing as the shock of death.

The entire throng of people began to cheer. Spontaneous psalms of praise echoed from both the travelers and the mourners. And everyone wanted to get a glimpse of my living boy and the remarkable rabbi.

In the chaotic celebration, my boy was almost forgotten. We smiled because he became impatient, motioning that he needed help removing his grave clothes. A friend hesitated, unsure of how tradition would tell him to handle this. Then, realizing there was no precedent for touching a *living corpse,* he stepped forward to help free my son. Others scrambled to join in, helping him to his feet so that he could stand and face the Lord of life.

Rabbi Jesus extended his arms to embrace the joy of my heart. They smiled at each other. Then my son and one of his friends each grabbed one of Jesus' arms and thrust them in the air as though he were the victor in a great wrestling match. Everyone cheered.

That moment I knew this young rabbi was *the Elijah who was to come.* I could identify with the widow who lived in ancient

[16]Psalm 16:10
[17]1 Kings 17:7-24

Zarephath in the prophet's day.[17] I know the sadness that ached in her heart when she lost her boy in death. I also know the joy she felt when the prophet thrice prevailed upon the Almighty to restore life to the child. And I know it was no coincidence now that Rabbi Jesus said the same words once spoken by the great prophet to me: "Woman," he said, "here is your son."

That day changed my life. From that day I cherished every moment that my son and I were together. And I have never forgotten that God's plan is far better than any plan we could ever conceive. Even when things turn completely against us, the Almighty has his way of turning evil to our good.

My son and I listened for news of Jesus' movements, even when his popularity waned. About two years later, we learned that our Rabbi had been crucified in Jerusalem, the victim of an angry mob. Eyewitnesses said that he bowed his head to speak to those who stood at the foot of his cross. His own mother was among them. His friend John was there as well. The dying rabbi said something that sounded very familiar: "Woman, here is your son." I was not surprised. My son and I had already had firsthand experience with this man's boundless compassion.

But with the news of his execution also came news that his body had not remained still and lifeless in the grave. The reports said that three days later, he arose to life, the champion over his own grave. We were not surprised by that either, nor did either of us ever doubt that it was true.

Today cases of demon possession make the news,
and stories of dark supernatural powers ensure
box office returns for the film industry. We get
a more sobering view of the power of evil from Scripture.
Gospel accounts remind us of Christ's dominion over all
things, including the forces of evil. But these accounts
also serve as a solemn reminder that Satan prowls
our world with deadly power, seeking to drive
a wedge between us and God's eternal love.

The testimony that follows is that of a witness who
personally experienced the dark estate of demon possession.
It is imagined testimony. But we note the chilling
reminder that evil is not a game and that the evil one is not
a boogeyman. Those who fail to heed warnings from God
will forever lose their souls to the powers of darkness.

——————— **Legion**[18] ————————————————

Just exactly when my body was no longer my own I cannot say. I cannot point to a day or an hour. I only know that my mind and heart were opened to that profane presence when I was still young. I became intimate with the darkness in my youth. That may not always be the way it is with demon possession; it was in my case. How I wish someone had warned me! I do not enjoy talking about this part of my life. But to understand my release, you will need to see the depth of my fall into hell.

For me, it began with curiosity; call it an overactive intellect. Human knowledge—the kind of information that is limited to our understanding of time and space—was never enough. Like Eve, I wanted to know the unknowable things that only God knows. I thought that if I knew both good *and* evil, I would become godlike. My weakness became an obsession.

In a perverse way, I got what I was after. But it turned out to be a lie; I became a god only to myself. I learned too late that self worship is a sign that the evil one has already established a beachhead on one's soul.

I found a power that is innately evil. I became obsessed with having it. With such power I believed that virtually nothing lay beyond my reach. I took up the "dark arts" and learned magical incantations and rituals.

The black arts drive men to perverse acts. People do unspeakable things in the name of everything that is unholy.

[18]Luke 8:26-39

My rituals demanded human suffering. As Satan's disciple I never gave the pain I was inflicting on others a second thought. Instead, I found power in it.

But I learned very quickly that the power that comes from evil is merely bait. Like some great serpent devouring its prey, evil eventually ensnares its victims and eats them alive. Satan waited for the opening. And soon I was eager to invite him into my heart.

Any distinction between *obsession* and *possession* is difficult to make. One does not merely play with the occult. Dabbling in the arts and lying prostrate at the feet of the lord of the dung heap are, in the end, one in the same. Beelzebub takes over with blinding speed and uncanny deftness in those foolish enough to believe the nonsense that evil powers are merely entertaining.

As I think back, I now realize that there were things I did that contributed to the power Satan had over me. I chose, for example, to inhabit burial chambers and tombs. This was in keeping with my conviction that death was not an enemy but a friend. The evil one wants everyone to believe this lie. I became comfortable living there among the dead. Even the sickening smell of death appealed to me. By surrounding myself with death, immersing myself in it, I became a walking tomb and a partner in the beast's perverse habit of turning truth inside out. Life is good—a gift from the almighty El Shaddai. I know that now. But I did not believe it then. Satan spun his lies and declared life worthless and death meaningful, even desirable. Satan, or Beelzebub, the lord of the dung heap, had control of my life.

My second conscious choice was to remain naked. It was a statement of sheer defiance, signaling my rejection of even the simplest rules of social order—a declaration that I had become a valueless creature—*subhuman*. It celebrated my own arrogance, my primal debasement, like Cain of ancient times. When God asked him "Where is your brother, Abel?" Cain's answer came without remorse: "Am I my brother's keeper?" God's judgment was unambiguous: "You will walk the earth a marked man, alone and restless." My nakedness was my mark. Now listen, I know what I am talking about. *Be careful of what you celebrate, what you applaud, what you encourage. If you choose to celebrate the darkness, you will be doomed to live in it.* I chose darkness.

Satan isn't just a powerful force; he is the father of lies. He offers something he was never empowered to give. He opposes the truth, falsely accusing the righteous. He diabolically tempts people to abandon their trust in God. He undermines the workings of God's Spirit, sowing weeds among the good seed. He enjoys ruining souls by attacking bodies. He was a murderer from the beginning. He haunts secret and forbidden places, waiting to pounce on the weak and fragile. He delights in inflicting pain and suffering. He masquerades as an angel of light and hides in waiting, hoping to invade the hearts of the faithful. He is the great liar, who declares himself the victor. That is his lie. He stands arrogantly against God and insists that all dominion, authority, and power are really his. He works tirelessly, trying to convince us that happiness is not found in what a gracious God has done for us but in the things we can gain for ourselves by what we do. He whispers in our ears the lie of the fundamental question in life: "Will it benefit me?" But instead we should ask, "Is it right?"

The devil is a fact of life. His power is deadly. Possession by his power is real. Temptation is real. Sin is real. Hell is real. His devastating power far exceeds any power we possess in and of ourselves. It is a mistake to underestimate the liar's capacity to destroy. It is a terrible error in judgment to believe that one can handle spiritual realities with human knowledge and earthly power.

On the other hand, it is important that you are not left with the impression that mine is a tragic story. These terrible forces have been trumped. There is a power far greater than the liar's. It is truth. And it too is personal. Though *my story* began with the liar, *my life* began with truth.

I owe my life to God's Son, *Jesus Christ*. What a thrill just to repeat his name! Satan and his followers hate the name Jesus because it is the name above all other names. He is El Shaddai: God above all other gods—the Almighty, whose blessings pour forth in immeasurable and unending love.

I can still picture the day so clearly. As Jesus' boat approached the rocky shore, I could already sense the demons stirring a great turbulence within. As he stood there on the narrow shore looking up, they gnawed at the edges of my soul like rats at work on a rotting corpse. Jesus searched the caves and tombs that pitted the steep face of the cliffs. My demons knew it. They knew who he was even when I did not. They knew his name, his power and authority. They knew his Father. They knew his purpose in coming to that desolate shore of Galilee's lake. Their groans were vicious and hateful. But an uncharacteristic terror rattled in their multiple voices as they drove me to my knees, screaming for mercy: "What do you want with me, Jesus, Son of the Most High God? I beg you, don't torture me!"

Imagine! Hell begging for relief! After all the suffering the demons had caused, they were still pleading with Jesus to lighten their punishment. What gall!

The closer Jesus came, the more enraged that company of hell grew within. I had experienced violent outbursts many times before, so violent that people considered me dangerous. They tried to protect themselves by chaining me to rocks. My demons were always too powerful. Time and again I smashed the chains and fled into the lonely darkness.

Now Jesus was the object of the demons' scorn. They flung me down the steep embankment, screaming vile obscenities in languages unknown to me. I hurled dirt and stones in his direction and smeared dung on my chest and face. Then I slashed my flesh on the sharp rocks until blood flowed.

Judgment came without hesitation. "What is your name?" demanded Jesus. His words struck a sharp body blow, rendering the demons powerless.

"Legion," came the hateful reply. The demons spoke with a single voice but were at one anothers' throats, hating each other as much as they hated Jesus. How quickly the alliance of evil is shattered in the face of pure righteousness! Finally their self-loathing manifested itself in utter despair.

They threw me prostrate at Jesus' feet, my body writhing violently in convulsive spasms. "Have mercy," they begged. "Do not order us into the Abyss." The spirits knew the torment ahead. They understood the eternal darkness that awaited them. And they dreaded it with all their being.

But God's time for binding Satan and his spirits in the eternal night would wait. Their judgment would come only as an expression of God's will, not theirs. The chains of infinite punishment would be held in abeyance. That time would come soon enough. For now Jesus would meet their pleas with a judgment more limited to time and space.

A herd of swine rutted about in the sand on top of a nearby ridge. Legion's voices begged Jesus to let them inhabit the pigs after they had been cast out of my body. They didn't have to wait long for an answer. In the blink of an eye, I was purged.

The swine bolted for the crest of the cliff and plunged headlong into the water below. For days their bloated bodies bobbed gently in the dark water along the lakeshore—a fitting new house for the raging legion of wickedness and evil! When the Son of God stands in judgment, the results are profound and just.

No one needed to tell me what had just happened. I knew the great miracle God had accomplished in me. The pall of evil had been lifted, and I breathed in the fresh air of life again.

I looked into my new master's face. There, in his gentle countenance, I saw righteousness. He had just snatched my soul from the gates of hell, and now, for the first time, I knew real security, not only in his power but in his love as well. Especially in his love. I sensed that nothing could ever pry me from the Father's loving arms again—neither death nor hell's power nor legions of demons!

Jesus instructed his followers to help me clean up. I bathed for the first time in many years. Someone covered me with a clean robe. We talked. I jabbered on, recalling every detail of the miracle. How happy I was! The dead no longer held my interest. Every part of me tingled and throbbed with new life. Villagers hurried to see if the news of my exorcism was true. Superstition clouded their thinking. They did not understand. They were afraid of the one who wielded so much power over evil. They feared the reprisals of the beast. Satan's lies had them convinced that evil could still triumph. They had been conned by hell's false promise of power. I wished that someday they too would realize that the truth stood there that day in the flesh and that he was already victorious in the great battle.

Jesus looked as though he wanted to stay and teach the people who had gathered. But they threatened him, demanding that he depart. It was in his best interest to go.

As he climbed back into the boat, I was prepared to leave with him—to remain at his side, a living tribute to the one who faced hell for me. I belonged to him now—his servant to do with as he pleased, though nothing I would ever do could repay him.

He looked at me one last time. His loving eyes told me that my shame was forever gone. The forgiveness in his look transported me beyond this life into eternity; I no longer felt dirty. The terror of my night had turned to day. The Prince of heaven had dismissed the prince of darkness with his eternal light.

"Go home," he said. "Tell everyone what God has done for you."

That is what I did. It is what I have been doing ever since. It is what I do even now as I give my testimony. Every word of it is true. I swear by the holy name of El Shaddai.

*Some maintain that meaningful dialogue is a thing
of the past. They argue that people have become
so self-indulgent that they are no longer interested in
hearing someone else's ideas or experiences. This theory
is interesting but debatable. People talk about
many things. Still, conversations rarely include
topics that touch on matters of faith. In the stewpot
of racial, ethnic, and religious diversity that
is America, the risks are too great.
As a result, people often forfeit conversations
that are truly important.*

*In the following testimony, ethnic and religious tensions
provide the background for a meaningful conversation.
If the witness were able to share her experience with us,
she would be the first to tell us how undeserving
she was to have been drawn into this remarkable
conversation—a conversation that was
the beginning of a joyous spiritual journey.*

A Conversation between Strangers[19]

Please, pardon the smile. I mean to offend no one. These proceedings have my highest respect. The call to testify is an honor—a privilege. I am grateful for the opportunity.

People are sometimes put off by genuine joy. I have been told that my winsome face is offensive, at least to some. I cannot erase it, nor would I ever wish to. It reflects the happy song that lives within me. I celebrate the person I have become, for I have feasted at the King's banquet table, and my thirst has been quenched with water from the springs of the Most High. I am now satisfied in serving him.

Do you wonder what gives me such joy? I have participated in the great harvest. Me, of all people! I was blessed with an opportunity to invite others. "Come and see" was my invitation. I gave witness to a town full of Samaritans. Though I remain nameless in your Bible, God chose me to play a key role in the first mass conversion noted in the record of his work on earth.

That is how it is in his kingdom: one sows, another reaps. He gives us our roles. We do our share—sanctified vessels, earthen pots filled to overflowing with his grace. We carry his living water here and there so that others may also be refreshed in the flood. But it is a rare privilege to see one's witness bear fruit as quickly or as abundantly as I did. Most blessed day! The people of Sychar came to Jesus because I invited them.

[19]John 4:4-42

But they also came to him in spite of me. What I am now is not what I was then. I have changed. Or maybe I should say *I have been changed.* I am different. People who knew me say that I have become a new person.

Before, every miserable detail of my manipulative, controlling history was public knowledge. I was a shrew. My reputation was widespread. The evidence consisted of five failed marriages. I take responsibility for destroying the lives of five good men. If God himself had not intervened, there would have been a sixth.

Perhaps my sudden change of heart was regarded as a sign. Perhaps that is what stirred their curiosity, if not their imagination. "Come and see a man that told me every evil thing I have ever done," I declared. It was an admission of guilt. But it was also my creed. "Decide for yourself," I challenged them. "See if this man isn't the Messiah promised long ago!"

And they did. The people of Sychar dropped whatever they were doing and ran to Jacob's well to find out for themselves. And when they had heard the master speak, their hearts were turned just as mine had been turned. Praise God! Like me, they concluded that there was more to this humble Jewish rabbi from Nazareth than met the eye.

We begged Jesus to stay with us in Sychar for a while longer. We wanted to hear more of his teachings.

And stay he did. Two days. Two more *blessed* days! And to think, it all began with a simple request for a drink of water!

Maybe that's the real miracle here. The event that changed my life was no more than a conversation—a few words. Nothing as dramatic as a war or a natural catastrophe or a life-threatening illness. No fanfare, as with a king's coronation. No outpouring of emotions, as with the tragic death of a loved one. Just words. But in that simple conversation with a stranger, I found my life.

The oasis always teemed with women in the early morning hours. They came to fill their clay pots. But they came more to catch up on the latest gossip than for the water.

I was not welcomed. I bore them no ill. I was, no doubt, a popular topic of conversation: *the man-eater.*

I cared little about what they thought or said, but I found myself drawing water during the heat of the day, when no one else was around. It was still four months before the harvest. At that time of year, the sun's rays are brutal by noon. This day I saw that I would not be alone while I did my work. A stranger sat nearby. He had the haggard look of a bone-weary traveler. The torrid heat had gotten the best of him. He was, no doubt, hungry and thirsty.

My eyes searched the ground, avoiding the unpleasantness of staring at a stranger. I watched him secretly though, keenly aware of his presence.

I thought the stranger might be Jewish—perhaps a holy man. If so, he was younger than most. The possibility amused me: a Jewish holy man traveling through Samaria!

It also made me uncomfortable. Jews despised Samaritans. Yes, the feeling was quite mutual. Jews thought of us as spiritual orphans—people lost and condemned in the eyes of the Almighty. They could not hide their contempt for us.

Long ago Samaria had given birth to a new religious perspective, blending Judaism with religions that respected the land and fertility and other natural deities. In those early days, many Jews living in Samaria wed *goyim*.[20] The bloodline became impure. To the Jewish mind, we Samaritans were half Jewish, half heathen, and totally unacceptable.

I presumed the holy man entertained that kind of prejudice. I did not know he had made a special point of sojourning through the heart of Samaria—that he had traveled here driven by his deep love for the lost. All I knew was that he was a Jew. You can imagine, then, how startled I was when he asked me to draw water for him.

"How can this be?" I wondered. I hesitated.

He sensed my confusion and responded in an odd way: "If you knew the gift of God," said the holy man, "and who it is that is asking you for a drink, you would be asking him and he would have given you *living water*."

---

[20]The Jews used the term *goyim* in a derogatory way in reference to all uncircumcised nations of people—heathens.

"What an air of self-importance!" I thought. Anyone could plainly see this fellow was nothing out of the ordinary. Furthermore, we were miles from the nearest freshwater spring. I wondered where he thought he was going to find this cool, refreshing *living water* of which he spoke with such confidence. Was he delirious? Or was this an example of Hebrew superiority? Had he forgotten that we shared a common ancestry?

"Are you greater," I asked, "than our father Jacob, greater than he who gave us this well and himself drank from it as did his children and their flocks and herds?" Joseph's tomb was but a stone's throw from where we were standing. If the stranger were a humble man, he would acknowledge that Samaritans had a right to lay claim to the same ancestral greatness that Jews claimed. This was a simple fact and common knowledge.

But the stranger's answer was anything but simple. And as to the matter of *greatness*, I think his answer was more like, "Yes, as a matter of fact, I am greater than Father Jacob." But what he really said did not have a hint of Jewish arrogance: "Everyone who drinks this water will be thirsty again, but whoever drinks the water that I give will never be thirsty again, for it will become the wellspring of life forever."

It was the word *whoever* that got me. In fact, that was the only part of what the stranger had just said that registered. *Whoever* spoke not of Jews or Samaritans but of *any* and *all*. I suddenly realized he was speaking with me on a level that transcended national politics or religious history.

For the first time in this quaint conversation, I dared to look into the stranger's face. I searched for something in his expression that might help me grasp the meaning of his mystical words and magical water. I found kindness and sincerity there, but not meaning. I could only assume he was speaking of water that had value beyond the boundaries of physical needs— water apart from human experience. I knew of no other kind of water. But the possibilities were intriguing. *Living water!* He certainly had stirred my curiosity. I wanted to pursue the riddle. Besides, I thirsted for conversation that rose above the mundane talk of weddings and burials, business transactions, and birthing techniques. At the very least, this talk of *living water* had promise as stimulating dialogue.

"Sir," I began, "give me this living water so I don't get thirsty anymore. Then I won't have to keep coming here to draw water."

The stranger squinted. He raised his open palm to shade his eyes from the glaring sunlight, scanning the shimmering horizon. The panorama he surveyed was the landscape of my heart. "Go," he demanded. "Get your husband and bring him back."

I was not prepared for this. The stranger's request was a compelling indictment, both offensive and convicting. *Get my husband?* What did this holy man know of me, my life, my disposition, my obsessions, my broken and desperate relationships? What did he know about my attitudes and what I planned to get out of life? The decayed condition of my heart was exposed—to a stranger. Like a master marksman, he had pierced the protective layers of my soul and penetrated my hidden secrets. Suddenly, unexpectedly, a complete stranger was forcing me to deal with questions of right and wrong. I had ignored such questions for too long. Now a stranger was forcing me to face my selfish life squarely. Soon I would discover that the well of my life had been poisoned!

I decided to be honest with this stranger, who peered into my soul. But honesty comes hard when one is accustomed to lies and half-truths. I could only bring myself to restate what I felt he already knew: "I have no husband." It was a half-truth. The relationship I was presently involved in was only half of a relationship, lacking the integrity of marriage. To be fair, it also lacked the love and commitment of two people who genuinely cared about each other. Frankly, I was using the man. The same could be said of all of my previous relationships. My relationships were always and only about me.

Thankfully the stranger did not seek a way around the truth. He was direct and purposeful, insisting on a conversation grounded in the unvarnished truth. But he pursued the truth with gentle tact, stating the facts. The strategy was disarming; the facts of our lives always convict us. "You say that you have no husband," he said. He made a point of facing me, of reading my eyes, of letting me know that honesty was the issue. "How accurate!" he continued. "In fact, you have had five husbands, and you are not married to the man with whom you are now living."

I flushed. Once again I found myself staring at the ground, this time to hide my shame.

"Sir," I answered, "I can tell that you are a prophet." (It was an old habit of mine—changing the subject. It always worked.) "Our fathers worshiped here on Mount Gerizim," I said. "I know that Jews believe the only place to worship Jehovah is in Jerusalem." I thought I might be more comfortable talking about other relationships, such as the relationship between Jews and Samaritans. Long ago Samaritans wanted to worship together with Jews in Jerusalem. But the Jews banned us from entering the Most Holy Place. So we built our own temple at Mount Gerazim and worshiped there according to our own customs and traditions. The topic seemed safe, and I was pleased with myself for stating my understanding of history in a way that would not offend a Jew.

The stranger quickly shredded any pretense I might have had in thinking there was no connection between worship and the condition of one's heart. "Woman," he said, "a time is coming when worship will no longer take place here or in Jerusalem. You Samaritans do not worship according to the Father's prescribed instructions. Jews do. The Jews have retained the many pictures of the Almighty's plan of redemption. Graven images erected in the name of religion here in Samaria have distorted the symbols of God's redemption. The time is coming—in fact, the time has already come—when the Almighty's own will worship him in spirit and in truth. Worship will no longer be conducted in a place. His own will worship in the intimacy of their own hearts, where no priest will be needed to mediate. The Father is only interested in the spiritual worship that comes from the heart, for God is spirit. Anyone who wants to worship him must approach his throne in faith with a repentant heart and an appreciation for the Lord's mercy."

If the stranger's earlier remarks wounded me with guilt, he now penetrated my heart with hope and promise. This was *living water*, I thought. And he was right; I wanted more. I wanted to be filled to overflowing.

"I know the Messiah is coming," I bubbled. I wanted him to know that I was familiar with some of those pictures of the covenant: the Pascal Lamb, whose blood was shed to save Israel, and the great Day of Atonement, when the sins of a nation were placed on the back of a scapegoat who was led into the desert. These were the Lord's holy pictures. They foreshadowed his deliverance. "When the promised Messiah comes," I added, "he will explain all of this to us."

But the stranger spoke one more truth—the greatest truth (if there is such a hierarchy), putting everything else into perspective. "*I am* the One," he whispered.

The One. I had not considered that possibility. It would have been too remote, too implausible, too unexpected. Who can imagine the Lord's deliverance appearing as a thirsty, hungry, tired holy man out here in the middle of nowhere? But that is what he said. "I am the One"—the promised one, the Messiah. He is the one for whom the eternal *I AM* had for centuries been telling Jews to look. Our sacred writings spoke of it too. But I, of all people, did not deserve to be here speaking to him. I was not a Jew!

Suddenly I understood what only moments earlier had seemed like foolishness. The confused conversation with this odd, worn-out stranger made sense. And his revelation gripped me with a kind of power I had never known before. This was not an empty intellectual exercise; he spoke to my heart, not my head. And what he said changed everything. What he said changed me.

There is no kind of change as powerful or dramatic or complete as the change that comes from drinking living water. I was so excited that I left my water pot there by the well and took a shorter route back to town, right through the middle of a grainfield. The crops would not be ready to harvest for some time, but the fields of the Almighty One of Israel were bowed and white with fruit. I had seed to sow among the people of Sychar, crops to cultivate and water, souls to gather in. I had reclined at his table, eaten his food, been refreshed in his fountain. Now I could not wait to get to work.

History is full of bizarre trials endured under unusual circumstances. Unlikely as it may seem, the courtroom drama that follows occurred in the shadow of the great temple in Jerusalem. The defendant is a woman. She is guilty beyond all reasonable doubt. The evidence is compelling. Her crime: adultery. The penalty required by law: death by stoning.

Now, two thousand years later, the accused finally takes the stand, but not to testify in her own defense. That has already been done. Her defender won her freedom before the only judgment seat that matters. Instead, she reads her testimony into the record in order to praise her defense attorney. True, it was he who exposed her sin to the light of the law. But it was the light of his eternal grace that proved to be her redemption. The transcript of her day in court is a reflection of his eternal, life-giving light.

Caught in the Crossfire[21]

I am surprised you want to know my story—a woman guilty of adultery. Yes, I was a woman guilty of destroying a marriage. But you still want to know how Jesus changed my life. You have asked me to describe the events of that day. You want my view of who I believe *he* is. I will tell you.

For days all of Jerusalem was asking that very question: "Who is this Jesus—this rabbi who turns everything upside down?" Some thought he was the Almighty's prophet—perhaps Elijah, returning in the same way that he had been taken up into the Father's bosom. A few even thought he might be the holy Messiah—Israel's hope of the ages.

His enemies argued that the Messiah had to come from Bethlehem; Jesus hailed from Nazareth they said. God's prophets never came from Galilee.

When it came to Jesus, it seemed everyone had an opinion. Except me. I didn't pay much attention. As far as I was concerned, the traditions of my people were more about eating and drinking. All the washing, sacrificing, and incense burning was completely lost on me. I never really understood the point. No one had taken the time to explain it. I simply never thought it was important. I was more interested in what I could get out of life. Do not misunderstand; I knew the rules. *Thou shalt have no other gods. Thou shalt not take the name of the Lord your God in vain. Keep the Sabbath Day holy. Honor your father and mother. Do not kill.* I understood what the Lord God had forbidden and the things he had commanded his people to do. I had decided it didn't matter. Life was too short to worry about some ancient laws imposed on us by a distant deity and enforced by a group of stuffy men. I had convinced myself that Moses had made it all up. The morning when I was caught in bed with the husband of another woman, I was merely living by my own rules. And the chief rule was "live for the moment."

Lying in bed with another woman's husband creates this distorted view of life. The *moment* becomes everything. I lived for the moments of sweet pleasure and arranged my life to find secret moments when I would not be caught. Like so many others, I did not realize that life comes with a contract. It holds us accountable for every moment that we are given.

So there I was, trapped in the storm of a sex scandal. The man—let me call him Joseph—had a wife and two children. He was a respected merchant, and he was the target of the other merchants. Certainly, I was hardly an innocent victim. The only difference was that he knew how to cover his tracks. Besides, it was common to hold a woman more accountable for the offense of adultery than her male partner, even though the Scriptures say both must share equally in the guilt.

But all that is beside the point. We were caught in the act. I heard the noise outside but did nothing. Joseph said we should not worry. Then they burst into the house, and all I could do was try to hide and make sure to cover myself. Joseph was gone in a flash, leaving me to face the intruders. They ordered me to dress, then dragged me out into the street. I thought they were going to stone me on the spot, but they pulled and pushed me down the street toward the temple. Pharisees always wanted everything done according to the Law of Moses.

The trial, as I imagined it, would be an attempt to embarrass Joseph; I was merely a pawn.

I already knew the charge and the verdict. It was the sentence that concerned me: stoning. But I had never heard of anyone being executed for this crime. The Law was rarely, if ever, carried out. Nevertheless, I would still face trial. Perhaps they would try to make an example of me.

When we entered the court of the women in the temple, one of them shouted about bringing me before the rabbi from Nazareth. I could see a small crowd gathered around this rabbi, listening to his lesson. The teachers of the law and Pharisees interrupted the lesson and stood me before Jesus.

There I stood before God and everyone else. Interrupting the rabbi in midsentence, "Teacher," said one of the Pharisees, "this woman was caught committing adultery. The Law says that such a woman must be stoned. What do you say?"

My trial had started.

I knew the man who stated the charges. I knew several of the others as well. They were scribes. Some belonged to the sect of Pharisees. I mean, I knew them *intimately.* How ironic that they would dare to indict me for adultery! They had apparently decided the little rabbi should serve as my judge. In fact, I quickly began to realize that it was the rabbi, and not me at all, who was really on trial. I was merely there to set the whole thing in motion.

He seemed only interested in going on with his lesson and tried to ignore the question of what to do with a woman caught in the act of adultery. He went on teaching, drawing a picture in the dust—a part of the lesson, no doubt. Anyone could see that he was not eager to be drawn into the case. It would put him in conflict with the Roman governor. Capital crimes were in Pilate's jurisdiction.

The Pharisees and scribes became angry at Jesus' lack of attention to them. They did not like to be ignored! These men were in earnest. They pressed the rabbi for a public opinion. The question was whether to follow Moses' Law to the letter or not. It was a trick. No matter how Jesus answered, he would end up looking bad.

The frightening thing was that they were right. The Law was absolutely clear on this point; I deserved to die. I knew that. The scribes and Pharisees knew it. Jesus knew it too.

He stood and looked each one of my accusers straight in the eye. "If there is one of you who is not guilty of sin," he said, "let him cast the first stone." Then he knelt and returned to the drawing he was working on in the sand.

The teacher's words brought an awkward silence to those who had brought me to Jesus. Perhaps he had managed to trouble their consciences, if such a thing still stirred within any of them. If they would have had so much as an ounce of the wisdom, every one of them would have knelt down and confessed his sins right then and there. Instead, one by one they slithered away. None, from the oldest to the youngest, was willing to risk further exposure.

But if the teacher's response was chilling for my accusers, it was devastating for me. Moments earlier I stood before a jury of men, convicted and subject to death by stoning. But the sentence Jesus had just spoken had the effect of convicting me in an even greater court. My offense was against God— against his holy Law: *Thou shalt not commit adultery.* Those were divine words. Moses did not invent the Ten Commandments. They were the Lord's words. They communicated his will.

Adultery is a crime of deception. It reeks of conspiracy— a sinister plot between two people who betray confidences and disguise the truth, who make a mockery of sacred commitments and unite on the basis of a lie. Moreover, adultery makes a sham of one of the most precious gifts that the Creator has given, the gift of one's own body. Mine had become a cesspool of iniquity. Even my own conscience, hardened as it was, found me guilty and condemned me to a punishment far more severe than my human accusers might have exacted.

I stood there shivering in the blazing sunlight, ashamed of my life.

My head said, "Run." And I could have. My accusers had disappeared. Their charges against me had gone with them. But I remained fixed in the judgment dock in which the temple crowd had placed me.

Jesus stood once again and faced me. The onlookers waited for his words just as I did. I trembled at his gaze.

"Woman, where are they?" he asked. "Is there no one left to condemn you?"

"No one," I said.

He smiled. "Neither do I condemn you. Now go and leave your life of sin."

My judge had spoken. I was free. He urged me to go. But I still could not get my feet to move. I stood riveted to that same spot, trembling, sobbing with remorse, relief, and a hundred other emotions. He finally had to say it again. "Go and leave your life of sin." And he indicated that I should be on my way.

Somehow I managed to drift out of the courtyard and into the open street, where merchants and peddlers mingled with the bustling throng of pilgrims. Guilty but suddenly free. Who could release a sinner like me from the just punishment I deserved? I wondered: "Who is this man who can dismiss the deep stains of a lifetime? By whose authority does he exhort me to leave my life of sin?"

I might still be wrestling with that question, except I returned. I wanted to thank the teacher for intervening on my behalf. As I approached, I saw that he was still teaching, just as he had been doing that morning. I overheard a portion of his lesson. *"I am the light of the world,"* he said. *"Whoever follows me will never walk in darkness, but will have the light of life."*[22] It was the answer to the question. He had even used the name that had been a part of Jewish history for thousands of years: *I AM*. When Moses had asked, "Who shall I say is sending me?" *"I AM who I AM"* was the Almighty's answer. Now Jesus said it in the same way: *"I AM."* Then he told his hearers exactly who he was: *"I am the light of the world."* His words connected my defender to the very beginning, when light first shined on all things created.

I testified earlier that I had never really been interested in much more than living life for the moment. That changed. I stayed on in the temple courtyard that night for the evening sacrifice. I had so much to think about. I had just spent the first day of the rest of my life, basking in the glorious light of God's mercy. I stood in his judgment hall where he defended me and

[22]John 8:12

acquitted me. It took some time to build a new life without Joseph and our secret meetings. Others continued to gossip for a time. I wanted to turn away from my life of sin. It mattered little. Jesus turned me around so I could start a new life.

The Jews called it the finger of God, the stroke,
or the scourge. We know it as leprosy. In the ancient world
it ravaged the body, poisoned the spirit, and
ripped every shred of human dignity from its victims.
There was no known cure. Death was imminent.
It usually came as a welcomed relief.

Jesus touched many lives during his ministry.
In one way or another, they all were the lives
of desperate people. None, however, was more desperate
than these pathetic figures forced to live in isolation
because the very sight of them frightened others.
They were the "unclean," who moved about
in the ragged shadows, like specters of the dead.
Jesus had compassion on them. He cleansed them
so they could return to their families and friends.
One of them now steps forward to publicly
thank his Great Physician.

The Gift of Moses[23]

I had ignored the sign—a white spot on my right forearm. Within a week or so, the infected area turned from fleecy white to a sickly yellow. The spot spread and reddened around the edges. A second, smaller spot appeared on my brow at the hairline. A few hairs on that spot also turned white.

People began calling the spots to my attention—as though I had not already noticed! Friends turned away when they saw me coming. I wrapped my arm and started to wear a turban to hide the mark on my brow.

The condition worsened. It clearly was more serious than a common rash. This was deeper . . . much deeper. A blood-tinged, watery ooze wept through the dressings. Dead skin fell off in the bandages whenever I changed them. The verdict was as sure as if the court had ordered me stoned. I was just as dead. The *scourge* had marked me for a bitter grave.

A fool might have continued to deny the facts. Not me. But there is a harsh difference between accepting a reality and being ready to deal with a reality. I was not prepared for the difficult times that lay before me.

Word of my condition spread quickly. My family embraced me, though not physically; that would not have been wise. They tried to prop me up with words of encouragement.

Tears were shed. They mourned as though I had already passed into eternity, shrieking the death song long into the night.

[23]Luke 17:11-19

I am a Samaritan. Jewish laws did not apply to me. If I had been a Jew, I would have been required to show myself to a priest. Moses had commanded this. The priest would declare me unclean. Then I would be banished from society and exiled from the Almighty's holy sanctuary, unable to worship in the Lord's house, not welcomed even in his outer courts.

No one argued when I said I must leave. It was a hard reality for them as well. But by remaining in their home, I would have been visiting a terrible hardship on them. The conversation of some members of the community was already turning ugly.

My spirit seemed to shrivel up and die when I had to turn my back to those whom I loved so dearly. Alone, I walked into the black, forbidding night that was my future.

I wandered into a Jewish community of about 20 people, all in various stages of the *living death*. I call it a *community*; it actually consisted of a few hastily thrown-together huts. Their only real purpose was to protect inhabitants from the blistering heat of the midday sun. The place lacked organization and planning. It lacked all those things communities normally have—marketplaces, roads, children at play. Nevertheless, this "community" became my home.

In the beginning the others disgusted me with their rank odors, hideous sounds, and repulsive, mutilated bodies. There is no way to escape the stink of death in an encampment of lepers. Whenever we could afford it, we mixed myrrh with olive oil, herbs, and spices to concoct an ointment. It soothed areas of exposed flesh, and the pungent aroma of the myrrh temporarily masked the stench of putrid bandages and rotting flesh.

I will never forget those days I lived as a leper. I can still hear the inhuman sounds. Leprosy attacks the mouth earlier than other parts of the body. The jawbone turns soft and brittle. Eventually the gums deteriorate. Teeth fall out. The tongue and palate lose their coordination and control, leaving a gaping hole in the face, drooling spit. Vocal chords become paralyzed. I can still hear the unearthly, hollow, body groans and guttural rushes of air gurgling through throats without palates.

Leprosy is even more offensive to the eyes. Hair falls from the head and eyebrows. Nails loosen and drop off. Oozing open sores and black patches of dead tissue invade large portions of flesh. Attempts are made to cover these open wounds with dressings, but it is impossible to completely enshroud a body with burial clothes before death has its final hurrah. Fingers, toes, and their adjoining joints rot away. The skin around the lips dries, cracks, weeps, then dies. It blackens, and the fleshy parts of the lips eventually fall away, leaving nothing in their place.

One man at the end of his life was maimed and immobile. Faceless. Voiceless. Limbless. His barely-human existence cast a shadowy picture of my future. The eerie projection left me physically sick, and I was unable to eat for several days. It took many more weeks for me to accept the fact that I was one of them, a *leper*—a term that honorable people refrained from using in polite conversation. People spoke of us as the *living dead*. And we were.

Jewish culture abhors death and filth. All the sacrifices and washings impress the need to be clean. Death is, after all, a part of the curse. Just touching a corpse rendered one unclean for 24 hours. Burials and executions were restricted to areas beyond the city walls. *The afflicted* were as good as dead. We were unclean and marked for death. The healthy made every effort to avoid us.

Our colony lay outside the walls of a small village on the Judean side of the border that separated Judea from Samaria. Fresh food and water were delivered each day to a drop point. We were hopelessly dependent, vulnerable. Marauders went out of their way to avoid us, but packs of vicious dogs and other wild animals were a constant threat.

I found an odd kind of comfort in the willingness of these people to accept me into their sad little band. I tried to help, tending the fire, changing wraps, washing those who could no longer care for their own needs. I did this in return for the human contact for which I still so desperately longed.

We followed Jewish traditions and laws. By law our clothing was a tatter of threadbare rags—a symbol of repentant hearts and the grief we suffered at the loss of our humanity. Hair (whatever there was of it) was to remain unkempt. We lived alone, each in a tiny lean-to hovel. The lower portion of one's face had to remain covered at all times. When we approached a village, we were to shout "Unclean! Unclean!" People would remain at a considerable distance, the space in between acting like some impenetrable gulf between the living and the dead. These edicts all came from Moses. I observed the Jews' laws and honored their traditions.

Time passes slowly in a leper colony. You try not to dwell on the suffering, though the obvious is unavoidable. You learn to share the misery. A fellow sufferer might say a few words of comfort and utter a short prayer with you. My friends taught me that the Almighty had made a special point of promising to make his presence known among the *living dead*.[24]

In the early evening hours, we would gather and talk. Sometimes the conversation would turn to our families and our life's work. Occasionally someone would dream of a miraculous cleansing—of Naaman, who had washed in the Jordan, or Moses, whose hand turned white with the disease. Then someone would recall the prescribed cleansing rituals that were required whenever a person had been cured.

According to Jewish law, a leper could only be readmitted into a community through a priest. A physician was rarely even involved. If someone actually were cleansed, it became a matter for the priests to consider. After seven days of waiting and observing, the priest was to offer four special sacrifices. We called these offerings "the gift of Moses" because they too had been prescribed in the Law of Moses.

The first was a grain offering—a simple ceremony. A small container of flour was offered up at the holy altar. This was a way of saying thank you to the Almighty. "How fitting!" I thought. The grain offering was not a bloody sacrifice.

The next three offerings required the shedding of blood. The guilt offering came next. This offering recognized that the individual had now been restored to full rights among God's people. He was cleansed and now permitted to once again worship in the holy sanctuary. He was no longer held guilty for the many years of inactivity. His failure to attend worship was fully forgiven, and his relationship with the Almighty was thoroughly mended.

The third sacrifice was a sin offering. This ritual brought the individual to his knees in repentance. It offered the complete assurance that every wrong had been atoned for in the blood of the sacrificial Lamb.

Last, the priest was to sacrifice a burnt offering. In this final act the cleansed rededicated the remainder of his life in service to the Almighty. This was a ceremony of reconsecration, symbolizing new life. After the offering he became a *living sacrifice* to the Lord. Only after all four sacrifices were completed could a former leper be free to reenter the mainstream of Jewish life and return to his family.

Interesting as the gift of Moses observance was, no one had ever heard of a single case of such a miraculous healing.

The kind people who deposited supplies near our camp served as our only contact with the outside world. Most of the news we heard was about family matters or events taking place within the village. One day we heard a rumor that a young, itinerant rabbi had cleansed a man whose body was covered with the disease. The rabbi had apparently sent the man to a priest with the instruction that the gift of Moses' sacrifices should be observed. The whole camp was stirred with a sense of hope. I was skeptical. In a few weeks the story was all but forgotten, and the stifling pall of despair hovered over the camp once more.

Then word came that the rabbi was on the move again, traveling in the general direction of Jerusalem but stopping here and there along the way. We could only hope that the route this rabbi took might bring him to the border.

Only a few days later, Jesus arrived, slowly making his way up the road that led to our village.

We helped one another to our feet—ten of us in all—and scrambled in the direction of the road. Along the way we agreed that those of us whose voices were still intact would plead for his attention.

A throng of people followed him. A dozen or so remained close at his side, deep in conversation.

"Unclean! Unclean! Unclean!" we cried. But our warnings did not slow his progress. Perhaps he had not heard us. Our rattling voices were so weak, so thin. His followers saw us. They were startled by the grotesque vision of ten *living dead* huddled among the rocks. They froze in their tracks, but the rabbi did not stop.

Instead, he shaded his eyes from the sun's brilliant light to look for us. When he saw where we were, he began to climb the rocky slope that separated us. He moved in earnest, closing the gap, coming closer than others would have dared. I suddenly felt the presence of the Holy One of Israel among ten of the *living dead.*

We shrank from his gaze, making every attempt to spare him from our hideous appearances. One of my companions was overcome with emotion. He sobbed out loud. The rest of us trembled in the holy man's presence. A few managed to say his name in unison as we had rehearsed. "Jesus." The plan called for us to communicate the message, "Lord, have mercy on us." The words poured forth all jumbled and confused. He understood us anyway.

He caught his breath from the climb and then took a moment to study each one of us one by one. "Go. Show yourselves to the priests," he said softly.

We looked at one another, wondering if we had heard him correctly. Then, as if they were afraid the rabbi might change his mind, a few of my companions bolted down the hill, or hobbled in whatever manner their fragile bodies still permitted. The rest of us tripped along after them in what amounted to a stampede of ten cripples. Ecstatic. Jubilant. Bounding and limping and clomping down the road together.

I was not the first to notice the change. We soon discovered that our bodies had been made whole. Diseased limbs were restored. Faces glowed, pink and healthy. Voices were able to speak. Someone began to sing.

How eager we now were to show ourselves to the priests! How satisfying the days of purification would be, even for an uncircumcised Samaritan! How good it would feel to return to my family and friends healthy and vibrant, no longer a threat to my community.

It was then, in our eagerness to get to the temple in Jerusalem, that I began to reflect on the required days of celebrating the gift of Moses. I remembered the significance of each of the four sacrifices. Something was out of place, or badly misplaced. It was the grain offering—the offering of thanksgiving. That was a first priority. In our haste we had forgotten to express our gratitude to the rabbi.

I argued that we needed to return to say thank you to him, to acknowledge his power, to recognize his compassion. How much time could it take? Let the priests make the appropriate sacrifices according to the gift of Moses' ritual when we got there. Surely the covenant law must be observed. But for now there was something more urgent to be done.

My friends would hear none of it—not from a Samaritan. The temple priests still had the authority to refuse to give us the gift.

I was disappointed that the others would not join me. I did not care. I only knew what I had to do. I turned away from my dear company of lepers. I became a majority of one and headed in the opposite direction, back to Jesus.

When I got to the village, I found a small crowd milling about Jesus and his friends. My presence still made people uncomfortable. When I hailed him, he stopped and waited for me to catch up. I threw myself at his feet to show him how grateful I was. I would have given my life for his. Only later did I realize that what I had just done was a burnt offering—a commitment to serve him with my new life. I could do no less.

He put his hand on my shoulder. "Rise," he said. He helped me to my feet. In his face I saw the sad look of disappointment. My companions had broken his heart with their thanklessness.

"Were not ten cleansed in all?" he asked. "Where are the other nine?" He was used to being treated this way. Then, to no one in particular, he looked about and added, "Did no one but this Samaritan come back to praise the name of the Almighty?" Others may have heard in his words an indictment of his own people. I heard the commendation of my great healer.

"Be on your way," he said. "*Your faith* has made you well."

My faith? I had never thought about my faith before. He disappeared into the crowd before I could ask what he meant. But the rabbi's words lingered in my heart.

Since then I have thought often about my faith. Everyone should. I once trusted my body to carry me through life. It was faith misplaced. As one of the *living dead,* confidence in my body shattered like a cheap clay pot. When faith is poorly placed, one's eternal destiny will end in a dry heap of lifeless dust outside the city walls. Money, friends, power, intelligence, the stars—we all put our trust in something or *someone.*

Whenever I have wondered about my faith, I think of him— the Jewish rabbi. My confidence now rests in him. It was he who cleansed me so thoroughly that I might some day stand whole and free of blemish in the presence of the Almighty. If he can do that, he can do anything.

Memory is one of the Creator's greatest gifts to mankind.
No other creature has the ability to appreciate history,
collect stories, or plan for the future by recalling the past.
We go to great lengths to preserve our past.
We honor those who came before us by remembering them.
Conversely, to be completely forgotten
is considered a disgrace.

To be forgotten by the Almighty, on the other hand, is hell.
Here is the testimony of a man who thought
God had forgotten him. Yet his life intersected with the life
of a man named Jesus on a day when both men's lives
slowly and painfully drained away. If it were possible
for our next witness to speak to us today,
he would remind us that being remembered in eternity
is far more important than being remembered in antiquity.

Confessions of a Dying Man[25]

Almost nothing about my life is worth remembering. No heroic acts. No deeds of kindness. No monumental achievements or memorable contributions to humanity. Even the Sacred Text mercifully declines to reveal my name, referring to me only as a common outlaw. I am happy you know so little of me. I lived in the shadows all my life. Whatever name I went by then no longer matters. Neither does my life of crime. So many things in my past I would prefer forgotten.

On that Friday morning it was not the wrongs of my life that bothered me but the fact that I had been caught. Don't trouble yourself speculating about my rebellion. I could have been put to death a hundred times over. And, for the record, not one of my lawless acts was committed for a noble cause. There is no honor in crime—even when committed against an oppressive master. Crime is crime. Putting a romantic spin on criminal behavior distorts the whole concept of law and order.

My life was a disgrace. I lived above the law. No parents, no law, no human authority, and no God would stand in judgment of my actions. The whole idea of being held accountable to some higher authority seemed absurd. My highest value was the freedom to do as I pleased. And I exercised such freedom with all my will.

As the sun dawned that day, I lived in the hope that everything would still work out—that I might yet miraculously escape execution. A reprieve perhaps. The idea was not that

[25]Matthew 27:33-50; Mark 15:22-37; Luke 23:32-49; John 19:16-37

remote. That very day, a fellow named Barabbas walked away from his own execution a free man. Unexpected things do happen. And, as the saying goes, "Hope springs eternal."

For me at the time, hope was only a lottery ticket—a wild card that might one day appear but most often did not. But one can never have enough of it. Hope provides a sense of momentum, giving pace and rhythm to life. With hope there always is a future—a chance.

But the human mind is capable of fabricating its own sense of hope. Counterfeit hope works against us. Like a bank account flush with cash, it creates false security, causing us to put off thinking about things that are inevitable.

Death is inevitable. By execution, by accidental cause, by disease or illness, in combat, or from the aging process, we all must face it sooner or later. We may escape its icy grip once, or even twice if we are lucky, but in the end we will all succumb. It is the inevitable consequence for failing to meet the standards set long ago by the almighty Creator. Scripture is brutally blunt on that score. From this side of the grave, in death there is no hope, for death extinguishes the promise of a future.

The seemingly endless succession of sunrises and sunsets of a lifetime lulls us into believing it will never end. We begin to imagine that we might be the one exception to the rule. We think, "Perhaps the grim reaper will pass me by" in spite of all the evidence to the contrary. Oh, how we want that illusion to be real!

I clung desperately to my false sense of hope. I could survive the pain. I would recover from the indignity of being stripped naked in public. But the thought of dying—the idea that my life would cease—was counterproductive. I had to work hard at putting that notion out of my head.

Then I heard the hammerblows and the screams. When it was my turn, I screamed and fought too. The first spike drove pain down my arm and shattered any lingering hope I might have had. I finally tasted the inevitable. As the feverish agony of creeping death set in, I found myself looking deep into the dark void of my own soul. I began to see all that I might have been. But the reality was all that I had become. Where there might have been a life well lived, there was only a record of crimes. My years had not been so much spent as wasted. Worse, I had thoughtlessly violated the sanctity of other people's lives: their properties, their rights, their good names, their bodies. Never once had I given anything back, except to exact revenge. Now it was *my life* that slipped away with each hour—not someone else's. How one's perspective changes! A shroud of self-pity drifted over me. Slowly I began to accept the fact that I would not live to see another sunset.

You cannot imagine the brutality and agony of crucifixion. I hung from the cross to serve Rome's view of law and order. I was not hanging in some forgotten and desolate frontier but along the public road so everyone could see. I was a public spectacle—Rome's way of making a brutal point to vanquished peoples: if you do these crimes, you will die in the same way. All Roman crucifixions attempt to make the same point. There may be other more horrible ways to die, but it would be difficult to overstate the suffering involved in this form of execution. The soldiers went through the motions of making the event more humane—a chunk of myrrh dissolved in a bowl of vinegar. It dulled the mind, but not for long.

The desire to die quickly gives way to the idea of having an end to suffering. Under the right circumstances death becomes an attractive alternative. The pain can become so intense that the idea of finding relief soon dominates every thought.

Shock sets in rapidly when one is suspended between heaven and earth by three angry nails. Pulled downward by your own weight, thirsty, struggling to gasp for one more breath, and profound pain—they all work together to disrupt your desire to live. Shock is a blessing. I slipped in and out of consciousness. My body shivered in fevered waves. Teeth chattered uncontrollably. Muscles twitched and quaked. But, nailed in this awful way, it takes a long time to die. Time to think. Time to have regrets. Time to fear the future, when you stand before God.

An eerie stillness settled in over the city. Thick, dark clouds towered in the west. The sun hid its light. I became acutely aware of an overpowering sense of loneliness.

Human vultures gathered to jeer us. They buzzed about the crest of Skull Hill like flies on a dead carcass. The earth's scum takes perverse pleasure in the suffering of others. None came to mourn my death or remember my life. My only companions were the other two who knew the same agony that I was experiencing.

The man hanging on the cross next to mine—the center cross—took the brunt of the crowd's mockery. Its ridicule played off of the shingle fastened above the man's bloodied head. It made some ironic reference to him as the *king of the Jews*. Whatever it said enraged the jackals.

To my shame, I added my own bile to the man's suffering. I was so used to lashing out at everyone and anyone. He was just a target for everyone, including me. He just happened to be available, and the only emotion I could feel any longer was bitter hatred.

But I also felt that I knew him, or at least I knew *of* him. A few days earlier I had stood near the city gate, where a crowd gathered. There a spontaneous procession made its way through the busy streets. The parade was carried along with the overtones of a religious pageant. People sang. They carpeted the path with palm branches and waved palm banners as if to welcome the return of a conquering hero. The children shouted: "Hosanna, hosanna to the Son of David. Blessed is he who comes in the name of the Lord." Then I saw the object of their affection. It was this same fellow, *Jesus*. He rode a donkey and blessed the people as he passed by—a pauper's king. I remember thinking that this rabbi from Nazareth was a shabby pretender to David's throne, if that was his purpose. Now he hung suspended on a Roman cross, and a cruel wooden throne it was. Mute. He appeared even less like a conquering monarch now. His popular support had all but vanished. He had just as little going for him as I had going for me. Today would also be his last on this miserable planet.

There were some prominent individuals among those keeping the deathwatch—men of rank and influence—priests, scribes, and Pharisees. They despised him for saying that he was God's Chosen One. Their ridicule was unrelenting, as though they considered his suffering a personal triumph. Jesus called out, "I thirst." Someone saturated a hyssop in vinegar, stuck it on the end of a stick, and waved it in front of him. A big soldier spat at him and played to the crowd with mocking sarcasm: "If you are the king of the Jews, save yourself." His antics earned him a laugh and started a new round of scornful comments.

There was plenty of acrimony between the Roman soldiers and that pack of religious hyenas. But in spite of their hatred for one another, the crowd's contempt for Jesus gradually blended together until it sounded like one infernal voice. It now focused all its derision on the center cross, treating its victim with the dignity of a worm. This meant they all but ignored me.

I strained to get a better look at the object of their intense loathing, clearing away the fog of pain so that I might make some sense of the issues. I was appalled by what I saw. His face was barely recognizable as human, already masking the pallor of death—a swollen, matted ooze of blood, perspiration, and spittle mingled with hair and dirt. Someone had planted a thorny crown on his head. It worked its way into his brow, just above the eyes. Shredded strips of flesh hung from his flanks. Every bone in his arching chest was visible. A pale tongue lolled between bloodstained teeth, wagging involuntarily as he labored to breathe. His eyes sunk deep into hollow, dark sockets. They betrayed his exhaustion and the same haunting loneliness I embraced. In horror, I wondered if I looked as broken.

I wanted to say something to validate my humanity—to give dignity to the bitter ending of our lives. I half considered asking him to take me along with him, wherever his future lay. It seemed like a foolish request—the incoherent babbling of a man in torment. But before I could shape my thoughts, the third victim's voice rang out with another insult: "Aren't you the Christ? Save yourself and us!"

The contrast between this Jesus and the two of us was suddenly hard to avoid. His punishment was not just. I was indignant over the comment. The remark made a mockery of God's Christ, something I was unwilling to do even in my final hour. It was blasphemy. I had spent a lifetime defying the Almighty's divine authority over me, but that and denying his eternal existence are two very different things. Besides, there was something about the man on the center cross that was impossible to dismiss. In his dying moments he had expressed tender concern for the welfare of his own mother. He had prayed that his executioners might be forgiven. I heard him. These were acts of kindness and love. It meant that he was more than just an ordinary man.

I spoke in his defense. "Don't you fear God?" I asked. "You and I were sentenced for a just cause. But this man has done nothing to deserve such punishment."

My own words convicted me. I had lived for myself; this man of God had lived for others. I had wasted my life; he lived with purpose. I cared about no one; he cared even about his bitterest enemies. I was evil; he was good. I was guilty; he was innocent. A profound conviction was forming in my dying heart that I cannot explain. For those who know God intimately, no explanation is necessary. For those who do not believe in God, no explanation is possible. The words I had been shaping earlier now boiled to the surface like a prayer of desperation. Imagine, me *praying!* With hands nailed awkwardly stretched heavenward, I made supplication to a dying man. How ridiculous to most who watched! But it seemed like the only thing—the right thing—left to be done. "Jesus," I pleaded, "remember me when you come into your kingdom."

The words barely escaped my parched lips, but I had finally found a way to express the hope of a lifetime. In some secret chamber of my heart, I still wanted *life* with purpose, free of guilt, in which heartache and pain are forever banished. More than anything, I still dreamed of reconciliation with my Creator.

It was a small thing to ask and a great thing as well—just to be remembered—not for the sake of posterity; it was far too late to worry about having a place in history. Besides, I wasn't interested in being remembered by just anyone, I wanted to be remembered by *him*, for he was not just *a* king; he was *my* King. I believed in his kingdom. His future was secure, having a spiritual history that stretched into infinity. My King had a future. Soon enough he would reign in a timeless, endless kingdom. I knew this in my soul. It filled my emptiness, satisfied my loneliness, and overcame my despair. To be remembered by this eternal King, that would be priceless.

My dying hope was not misplaced. "I tell you the truth," Jesus whispered (How could he have known that something as simple as the truth would mean so much to a dishonest man like me?), "today you will be *with me* in paradise."

That is my story! You wanted my statement. It can be summarized in two simple words: *with me*. There is no future without Jesus. To be with him *is* paradise. *With him* no man is alone. *With him* there is meaning and purpose. *With him* there is forgiveness. *With him* there is goodness. *With him* there is life and hope and a future.

You may find this hard to believe, but that day suddenly became the best day of my life. I had been handed a kind of reprieve that put all other reprieves to shame. Amid this torturous death, I found hope—not wishful thinking or positive optimism—real hope, hope that comes only as a gift from God himself. It was more than a lottery ticket. It was as good as gold—the gold of paradise.

I have one other memory of that remarkable day. Not long after our exchange, Jesus uttered a prayer of his own. It was a shocking thing to say. In sheer terror he shouted, "My God, my God, why have you forsaken me?" I shuddered at the thought. Human loneliness is one thing, but to be isolated from God is worse than death itself. To be *forgotten by God* is far worse than crucifixion. This dying Jesus felt the cold, hateful anger that God harbors against everything that is evil. No mere man could withstand that horror.

Then he spoke one last time. "Father, into your hands I commit my spirit." A sense of peace flashed across his pale countenance, and he willed himself into death's icy sleep.

The soldiers came with sledges to hasten death. Their purpose was to crush our legs. When they examined Jesus, he was already dead. A soldier lanced his side with a spear. Water and blood poured forth from the wound—convincing evidence.

Not long after that I breathed my last tortured breath. My position at the King's right hand was forever secure in death, even as it was in the last moments of life. You will remember me as the dying thief who, in the eleventh hour of his life, was handed the key to Christ's eternal kingdom. But it matters very little how you remember me or that you remember me at all. The stories of human history will someday pass into oblivion. Eternity, on the other hand, matters. To be remembered by an eternal God—that is everything!

The Greek historian Xenophon wrote, "Direction is left to the commander and execution to the soldier, who is not to ask why, but to do only what he is told." In the world of any military organization, nothing could be truer. Soldiers follow orders.

But what if a soldier receives an order that is patently unjust? The Roman centurion who is about to take the witness stand once received such a command. It changed his life forever. Moreover, the story he has to tell will begin to sound more like your own with each new reading.

A Soldier's Witness[26]

The *crime of the ages* some have called it. I was there. My face may not be familiar, my name may not ring a bell,[27] but I played a critical role in a historic execution. The testimony I gave then rocked the world. It still does.

I was a centurion—the backbone of the Roman army. Rome was the master of the civilized world—a military machine. The machine made the peace. The machine also kept the peace and exploited the peace.

We were the machine—soldiers like myself. Our blood and sweat was the platform for Roman might.

That day I awoke to a crowd of Jewish leaders making a commotion just outside the gates of the Praetorium. They had a prisoner in hand, calling it a capital case. These men were religious fanatics, loath to defile themselves during their Pesach by entering a gentile courtyard.

I had managed only a few hours of sleep, not enough to rise in good humor. This was a Jewish holy week. Insurrection was in the air. You could smell it. The Passover always brought pilgrims to Jerusalem. It brought thugs and hoodlums too. Several ugly incidents had already occurred. We expected more of the same.

My very first thought was about a zealot named *Jesus*. It was my habit to try to anticipate orders. I awoke expecting an order to crucify a fellow named Barabbas. Rumor had it that

[26]Matthew 27; Mark 15; Luke 23; John 18,19
[27]Tradition claims this centurion's name was Longinus.

Pilate's sentence would be finalized some time that morning—
on a holy day.

In this cauldron of rebellion, I could see Pilate's logic. Cruci-
fying a few of the extremists at the height of Passover would
send a strong message to anyone hell-bent on inciting sympa-
thizers to riot.

The crowd was already beginning to become ugly. It
wouldn't take much for this crowd to turn into a mob. Every
Roman soldier feared facing a mob. The mobs I had faced had
always turned into bloody exchanges between unarmed men
and my hardened armed men. I hoped we would not have
to face this crowd. When I arrived, Pilate had already taken
his place.

He sat in his chair, the picture of Rome's power and authority. I admired that kind of authority—so absolute, so sweeping
and broad. It was the thing about Roman rule I appreciated the
most. Roman will was like iron. Those who challenged it paid a
heavy price.

A slender, bearded man stood bound before Pilate. The governor listened to the indictment with measured indifference.
Everything about Pontius Pilate was calculated. The official
voice of imperial Rome was also the heavy hand of Caesar.
Pilate used that power to maximum effect.

The prisoner was submissive. There was nothing for me to
do but stand by and wait.

It was then that I noticed the accused was not Barabbas, as I
had expected. Nor was the charge murder. This man was being
indicted for sedition. And the leaders of the Jews were demanding death as his punishment. It was oddly out of character for
Jews to show an interest in supporting Roman domination.

On the other hand, the charges were vague. Pilate had no
interest in pursuing a case of trumped-up charges. One of the
members of their Sanhedrin shouted, "If he were not a criminal, would we have brought him before you?"

The remark irked the governor. It was a sarcastic attempt to
cast Pilate as the fool. I knew the rage within Pilate. I had seen
it explode before. But now his demeanor remained calm and

controlled. "You don't have a case!" he argued. These people always had a different way of interpreting Roman law.

The governor indicated that I should bring the prisoner inside, where he could question the man. I learned the accused was a Galilean and that his name was Jesus. He was from Nazareth.

Pilate did most of the talking. The rabbi made no effort to defend himself. I took this as a sign of either guilt or indifference. Perhaps this Jesus was eager to end his life. Maybe he was a sad fellow who had lost his purpose for living. I had seen it happen to soldiers. People having a purpose in life instinctively put up a struggle. Besides, there were other ways—better ways—to end life than dangling from a Roman cross.

I delivered a note from the governor's wife. Pilate read it, then handed it back. It warned him to avoid taking action in the case of Jesus of Nazareth. Pilate's wife had been frightened by a dream and was convinced that no good would come of this matter. If his wife's concern troubled Pilate, he didn't show it.

When I told the governor that Jesus hailed from Galilee, he immediately realized he had a way to escape this affair with a minimum of political fallout. "Isn't Herod here in the city today?" he asked. "If this man is from Galilee, he is under Herod's jurisdiction. Let Herod deal with him." Pilate was always delighted when Herod was left twisting in the politically charged winds of Jewish affairs.

I took a few men and marched the prisoner over to Herod's palace. But Pilate's strategy failed. The prisoner was back in my custody for the trip back to Pilate. Herod was too smart to let the governor shift this troublesome case on him. His court was more interested in being entertained. When Jesus did not perform whatever wizardry he was hoping for, Herod quickly lost interest. In mock honor, Herod's men wrapped the pauper's king in a dusty, regal cape and ordered me to return him to the Praetorium. The rabbi was still Pilate's problem.

The restlessness in the streets had escalated. Someone had been working the mob, prodding, inflaming hatred for Jesus.

An ugly incident was quickly degenerating into a full-scale political standoff.

I remembered Barabbas. It was customary for the governor to release a prisoner during the Jewish holiday—a gesture of goodwill. The governor was ahead of me, as always. His new scheme was to offer an execution to the bloodthirsty mob while, at the same time, manipulating the release of the rabbi from Nazareth. He wagered the Jews would opt for releasing the harmless rabbi instead of a murderous rebel. This plan was his trump card. But Pontius Pilate never left things entirely to chance. He saw a way to hedge his bet by ordering soldiers to flog the rabbi.

My men executed orders with brutal force and without compassion. We obeyed with unquestioning loyalty. It was not up to us to challenge the morality of a command. But even obedient Roman soldiers like my men recognized the injustice of this order.

I left the distasteful work to a muscular Gaul. We lashed the prisoner to a post. When all was done the rabbi's back and sides lay open, dripping thick, red blood. The sight and stink of the little rabbi-king turned the weaker stomachs of bystanders.

One of my men twisted a thorny vine into a crown. He drove it deep into the rabbi's skull with a stick. Another placed a reed in his hands—a mock scepter. What a pathetic picture this powerless king made!

The men took turns slapping the prisoner across the face. They bowed the knee, exclaimed "Hail, king of the Jews," and made bad jokes about his royal ancestry.

I encouraged this mean-spirited play. I felt no pity, no compassion, no remorse. It nurtured *esprit de corps*; it fostered a bloodlust. Both would come in handy if the game in Palestine turned more defiant. Then we would have to teach the Jewish population a painful lesson.

Pilate was impatient. He was also impressed with our work. We had turned this quiet, pathetic prisoner into a pulpy mass of sweat, saliva, and sticky, red ooze. It was difficult to look at the man without cringing in sympathy. That was Pilate's genius. He presented Jesus to the mob for a third and final time, offering it the rabbi or the murderous zealot.

"Give us Barabbas," screamed one of the mob's leaders. "Free Barabbas," mimicked the mob. Its cries echoed throughout the Praetorium.

"But here is your king," mocked Pilate. If the temple crowd could be ironic, so could he. He pretended to honor Jesus with an overdone dramatic gesture normally reserved for royal celebrity. "Look at him."

This was Pilate's undoing. The error was decisive. The people were waiting for Pilate to repeat the reference to Jesus' kingship. It gave them an opportunity to raise the stakes, declaring loyalty to only one king: Caesar Augustus. "We have no king but Caesar," they cried. What hypocrites! Of course, I couldn't imagine a Jew saying such a thing. But they hated Jesus even more than they hated Rome. The rabbi's fate was sealed.

The crowd began to chant rhythmically: "Crucify him! Crucify him!" The words became a throbbing, deafening din.

I was surprised at the way the crowd reacted to Pilate's offer. I was not at all surprised with Pilate's next move. He was completely predictable. He stepped over to a small fountain, trickling water into a basin. In it he symbolically washed his hands—another dramatic gesture.

I would be the last person on earth to ever suggest that Pontius Pilate had a conscience. Yet it was clear to me that he did not want to be held accountable for murdering this holy man, whom he considered innocent. The gesture absolved Pilate from nothing, but his political interests were served. It was his way of letting the Jews prevail momentarily without conceding any real power.

A woman screamed, "His blood be on us and on the generations that follow!" If Pilate heard the remark, he ignored it. The trial was over. He leaned in my direction and quietly said to me: "Release Barabbas. Then take this man outside the city and crucify him." When the people understood that the decision had gone their way, they cheered wildly.

The way to the execution site meandered along a narrow, cobbled path. We cinched the crossbeam to the prisoner's shoulders yoke-like in an effort to get him to carry the burden. That was impractical, at least for Jesus. He was in such a weakened condition that he toppled over every few steps.

Concern that this execution would linger on into the Sabbath was growing. I scanned the crowd, looking for someone we could recruit to carry the beam in place of the doomed rabbi. A fellow named Simon—I remember he came from Cyrene—met the need. We soon were moving again toward Golgotha with greater resolve.

The rabbi had a following. Along the route women sobbed over the brutal treatment we were giving their helpless king. When he passed the women, he said the strangest thing: "Daughters of Jerusalem," he began, "don't weep for me. Weep instead for yourselves. The days are coming when it will be said, 'Blessed are the wombs that never bore children and the breasts that never offered milk to an infant.' The day is coming when people will beg the mountains to crush them and the hills to bury them. For if they do these things in the season of a green tree, what will happen when it is dry?" At the time the rabbi's words sounded like fever-driven babbling. I let him ramble. But 40 years later, in my old age, I recalled these very words and wondered how he knew. For with my own eyes I saw the horror predicted by this man. Four decades later the Jews refused to knuckle under, so Rome crushed their city into a heap of powdery rubble. I still marvel at the rabbi's foresight.

A message arrived at the site about the same time that we were preparing to start the first phase of the crucifixions. Apparently Pilate was still bothered by the rabbi's case. He felt compelled to make his point again regarding the rabbi's claim to a king's throne, though to this day I remain puzzled as to the exact point Pilate thought he was making. His order was simple and was something we would normally do anyway. But Pilate wanted to make sure we didn't forget. The order was explicit and told us to tack the accusation to the top of the cross of Jesus. It read "Jesus of Nazareth, king of the Jews" in Latin, Greek, and Hebrew. Pilate seemed to want the whole world to know who this man was.

Some of the Jewish leaders were displeased with that wording. I told them I was under orders. A contingent of Pharisees went storming off to try to get Pilate to change it.

Protocol for crucifixion called for administering a mixture of gall, wine vinegar, and myrrh to the victim. It made the prisoners easier to handle. This action cultivated the illusion that Rome was a compassionate master. The rabbi refused it.

The quicker one can get on with these things, the better for everyone involved. My men knew what to do. The nails were set. All three crosses were secured in the rocky soil. The placard was fixed at the top of the center cross. We cordoned off a tight circle around the trio for crowd control.

Soldiers are paid not to think. We had a nasty job to do. We forced ourselves to ignore the suffering we were inflicting. We came expecting our victims to curse us. Before it was over, they usually did. Believe me, it leaves an impression when one of your victims says a prayer on *your* behalf instead. That is what the rabbi did. He prayed for us. "Father, forgive them," he whispered, "for they do not know what they are doing." That is what he said—"*Father, forgive them.*" I had seen and heard of a lot of strange things connected with executions, but I had never heard of this happening before.

I could not ignore it. When such a thing happens, one has to stop and consider it. *Forgive*—a warrior just doesn't hear that word very often. Yet when you have blood on your hands, it is important to contemplate forgiveness. I had a lifetime of shameful deeds desperately in need of forgiveness. Now this rabbi, whom I was executing, comes along and begs his God to forgive me. Come on!

We settled in for the long haul. Crucifixions can take days. The mob at this execution was particularly vile and contemptible. But they were not a threat. A few of the rabbi's faithful stood at a distance, afraid that someone might still connect them to their fallen messiah.

My men sat down on the ground, content to rattle their bones and gamble the rest of the day away. The rabbi's cloak was made of fine cloth and was woven in a unique, seamless pattern. It soon became the object of their game. As a soldier my convictions were actually quite simplistic. Life was a crapshoot—a simple throw of the dice. Every day could be my last. But dwelling on that theme can paralyze a person. So you learn to hope for the best. Maybe you will get lucky; maybe you won't. I'll bet there are people in your world too who simply walk through life with their fingers crossed.

But a soldier is also a realist; he knows that he must deal with facts. On that day some facts were hard to ignore. I was beginning to have difficulty reconciling some things to pure luck: the man's prayer on behalf of his executioners, the placard declaring him a king, the tone of the mob, and Pilate's eerie struggle over the man's innocence. I had overheard some of the Jews recalling a messianic prophecy that sounded strangely similar to this event. It was all too coincidental.

Around noon dark clouds filled the heavens like huge, angry fists ready to pummel Palestine. The sun disappeared. A profound darkness seemed to say that nature itself had gone into mourning. It felt as though all of the world's light had been extinguished.

In the suffocating black shroud that clung to the hill, the mood began to change. The mockery and derision ended. My men moved about in reverent rhythms. They spoke to one another in hushed tones. The rabbi was not afraid to die. But now there was terror in everyone else. Many left. One by one, they anguished over the day's events, beating their breasts in self-condemnation. Those who remained had second thoughts about the justice of this execution. I considered the possibility that we were putting an innocent man to death—the same conclusion Pilate had already arrived at several hours earlier. What good did such a conviction do for him?

While I stood there I was overwhelmed by a sense of remorse. I confess I was terrified over the possibility that we were murdering God's Son in cold blood. In him I could only see a magnificent goodness—a kind of goodness mortals are unable to generate—a divine innocence, if you will. I tried to think of someone I knew who possessed such qualities and could think of no one.

My own convicted heart was finally the engine that moved me to speak. "Surely this was a righteous man," I shouted. The reaction was spontaneous. It echoed in my heart. I suppose they were words of judgment—on Pilate, on the religious leaders, on the screaming mob, on anyone responsible for this outrage, on injustice of every kind, on myself. My declaration was an indictment of all those unrighteous acts that brought Jesus there to that terrible place. I said it loudly, with conviction. If I should ever find myself before a tribunal defending myself for what I was saying, I wanted plenty of witnesses so that the evidence would be irrefutable. I said it. "Surely this was the Son of God." I meant it. And I have never taken it back. I never doubted it. The man hanging from that cross was the Son of the almighty Hebrew I AM and truly the King of the Jews.

It haunts me to this day to know that I participated in his murder. But the moment I understood who he was and what he was doing, my heart was as light as air.

There was something too about the way this Jesus left life behind, like a child falling asleep in a parent's loving arms. "Father," he said, "I place even my soul into your waiting hands."

Then all hell broke loose. The earth began to tremble, and rocks split. For a time it was chaos, as though nature had arisen in profound upheaval at this crime committed against the Holy One of all creation. I was suddenly aware that the earth's quaking and heaving signaled the radical shift that was taking place in my own heart. I stood there in awe at the base of that awful tree, washed by the warm rain as it gushed from the sky. Twenty centuries of honest confession have not changed the simple fact that I helped kill the King of life. But there is a far greater glory in that fact: he died for me.

When I returned to Pilate to make my report, I could see that the rabbi from Nazareth was still on his mind. He inquired if the man was dead yet. When I confirmed it, Pilate introduced me to two men, both members of the Jewish Sanhedrin. One was named Joseph, from Arimathea, the other Nicodemus. I had not seen them earlier in the day, working the crowd. I concluded both were sympathetic to the rabbi's cause.

The governor ordered me to remand Jesus' body over to them for burial. We returned to Golgotha by separate routes. I wanted to be alone with my thoughts. Both of them seemed to want the same.

Have you ever looked back on your life and recognized key moments that made a difference? I am speaking about those earth-shattering moments that have made you the person you are. I think often about the few hours that I had the privilege of being close to my King. It was no chance meeting, no twist of fate. The order *"Centurion, crucify this man"* was the blackest moment of my life. But it was also the most glorious. In the aftermath of that command, I was forced to come to grips with the cold inhumanity of my own heart. In those same hours, I came face-to-face with the King, who had the power to penetrate the calluses of my heart and touch it where it would respond.

AFTERWORD

Perched awkwardly aboard a borrowed donkey, a pious teacher sets off down a pebbled path. His destination: Jerusalem—the city shimmering in the distant haze. A small band of men follows on foot. They have spent the early morning hours together on the Mount of Olives in a quiet spot overlooking the city. The rider lurches as his bantam mount rocks forward on the trail. He covers his head with a flaxen prayer shawl, a gesture of reverence and humility. The beast seems a few sizes too small for a grown man to ride. The rabbi's sandals nearly scrape the ground.

Some of the rabbi's disciples have draped their cloaks over the beast's back to form a makeshift saddle. The surefooted animal clickety-clacks its way down the rock-studded trail. It heads down from the Mount of Olives, down toward the main road that leads back up the opposite slope of the Kidron Valley to one of seven impressive gates.

Curious men and women are attracted to the little entourage. A few decide to join the group. A handful more join, and eventually the company resembles a troupe of pilgrims nearing the end of a journey. The mood is jubilant, almost giddy. Strains of a festive psalm fill the air.

In the gleeful spirit of the moment, a young man with his hands on his hips struts boldly in advance of his hero. His self-appointed role is to proclaim the approach of the Peasant-King. Another waves a palm branch in broad circles, pretending to wave the victory banner of a triumphant champion. "Blessed is the King!" intones someone in the crowd. "Blessed is the one who comes in the name of the Lord!" echoes the crowd. It chants the same phrases rhythmically back and forth. The people have heard and sung these very words many times before as a ritual part of their annual pilgrimages. Their music is amplified through the valley below.

Several women lock arms and dance to the cadence of the chanting. With a lilting two-step, the human chain shuffles its way down the cobbled slope. The spontaneity of their movements and the serendipity of their laughter delights everyone.

Children, drawn by the sounds of a celebration, are also assimilated into the crowd of happy pilgrims. Mothers follow at a distance. This is the first day of their workweek. They are invigorated by the joyous clamor—a welcomed respite to the monotony of their daily routine.

Boys cut palm branches and toss them onto the path. They have seen the grand entrances of Roman legionnaires garrisoned in the city—conquerors full of themselves and their adventures. These youngsters have paid homage before. But the growing assembly is more akin to a religious pageant than a military dress review. This is the first day of the Passover. It is a time to recall how God delivered his people from the oppressive hand of an ancient Egyptian pharaoh. Later in the week, in narrative and song they will reenact the night when lambs' blood spared Hebrew homes from death's icy grip.

More people collect along the route to get a glimpse of celebrity. When word spreads that it is the rabbi from Nazareth who is passing by, they throw their coats onto the dusty road, lending dignity and majesty to his otherwise insignificant appearance.

Most of the toddlers have learned the Hebrew word *hosanna*. Their serendipitous hosannas are sincere. They have a profound esteem for the unlikely hero gently swaying atop the burro. Holy men are accorded a high degree of honor and respect. "Hosanna to the Son of David!" the children sing. *Hosanna* means "save." It is a word generally reserved for use in connection with the promised Messiah—the one who would some day come from David's family line to redeem Israel. The expression recalls a happier time, when Israel was free from foreign occupation. *Hosanna* expresses the desire all people feel for deliverance from the difficulties and troubles of life. At the same time, this *hosanna* also hints of a grand and glorious future filled with the same kind of hope the ancient Israelites had as they left Egypt. The spontaneous congregation has somehow grown into a living tribute to the humble rabbi. The population is in need of a new hero. It celebrates Israel's champions in a quixotic blur of past, present, and future. Many hope their enthusiasm will ignite new passions and reinstate Jewish influence to levels that prevailed long ago in the days of David's kingdom.

As the throng bumps its way down the road, its number continues to increase. The celebration grows more animated and exhilarating. With the force of an old habit, grandpas and grandmas add a hearty *shalom* to the hosannas sung by the children. "Peace in heaven," says one old-timer. "Glory in the highest," sings out another. The blessing has been a constant of Jewish culture for centuries.

As they approach the city, several religious leaders—men of exemplary reputation and high calling—mingle with the crowd. They are spying on the activities of this rabbi, who rides a lowly donkey. Anyone close to the situation knows they are up to no good. They belong to a Jewish sect known as the Pharisees—the watchdogs of Jewish culture. These men occupy their time discussing law. They imagine their role in society as appointed judges. Their service to God, they believe, is to be living models of the Law of Moses—the Torah. For the last year they have dogged every step of the man who is, at the moment, being proclaimed the people's King. The good rabbi has apparently challenged the rules these men have so carefully nurtured and cultivated, even those beyond the Torah. Public admiration for this itinerant teacher who dares to question their authority is at an all-time high. They can no longer wait for his surging popularity to fade and disappear.

One of them works his way through the crowd. He maneuvers himself into a position near the rabbi. "Teacher," he intimates in a half-whisper, "rebuke your followers." There it was; an official voice had spoken. The Pharisee had not even bothered to fold his demand into the wrapping of polite rhetoric. His meaning could hardly be more explicit. Rabbi Jesus must now decide if he will submit to the will of the Jewish leaders or not.

The retinue pushes on, traversing a series of cobbled terraces leading up a graded embankment. The procession is now headed literally up to the city's walls. The crowd's momentum dictates the pace—a pace that demands progress—though no one seems to have given much thought to a destination. Perhaps the objective is the southern flank of the temple mount, where throngs of people gather to have their innocent, little, white lambs blessed for the Passover sacrifice. At any rate, the rabbi and the religious leader cannot stop and talk. The humble rider turns to acknowledge that he has heard the ultimatum. His carefully chosen words mark the boundary for the final conflict. "If my people keep quiet," says the rabbi softly, "these ancient stones will break forth in songs of praise."

And they would. This was not a blush of sarcasm from the Savior's lips; Jesus meant every word of his answer. He was stating a cosmic fact. One day all of creation would pay homage to the Lord of all things, including the stones being trampled by the beast whose burden was the King of life. The hills and the valleys and the stone walls surrounding the city would praise him. The Pharisees, whom Jesus had once called whitewashed sepulchers, would bow in honor. Their knees would bend, no doubt, grudgingly.

Moreover, our own once-lifeless hearts of granite will dance and sing to the music of our redemption. Our hearts will beat to heaven's consecrated rhythms. Won't it be grand? What splendor! There, in the new Jerusalem, we will be at the Lord's side, giving witness to his goodness and grace with our whole being. Your statement and mine will be placed into the living record as evidence, documenting our salvation in its most complete and permanent manifestation. What will the testimony of your heart prove? What will you say before the judgment seat of the Most High when it is your turn to stand in the dock? The apostle John had a preview. He saw witnesses come forward one by one to repeat their sworn testimonies for all creation to hear. The evidence is compelling. It echoes endlessly through the holy chambers of the Almighty's infinite hall of justice: *"Worthy is the Lamb, who was slain, to receive power and wealth and wisdom and strength and honor and glory and praise!"*[28]

[28]Revelation 5:12